The
European Community

THE EUROPEAN COMMUNITY

S. F. Goodman

St. Martin's Press   New York

All rights reserved. For information, write:
Scholarly and Reference Division,
St. Martin's Press, Inc., 175 Fifth Avenue,
New York, N.Y. 10010

First published in the United States of America in 1990

Printed in Hong Kong

ISBN 0–312–04882–3

Library of Congress Cataloging-in-Publication Data
Goodman, S. F.
The European Community/S. F. Goodman.
    p.   cm.
ISBN 0–312–04882–3
1. European Economic Community–Great Britain.   2. European
federation.   3. European Parliament.   I. Title.
HC241.25.G7G67   1990   90–8401
337.1′42—dc20   CIP

To HELEN, who encouraged me from afar

Contents

5 **Agriculture – Too Successful for Its Own Good?** 70

6 Economic Performance 91

7 **Money 107**

List of Tables and Figures

Tables

Figures

Preface

The European Community has an exceptionally good statistical office (Eurostat). Its publications are available in all good reference libraries. Eurostat has recently broken new ground with an excellent sixty-page illustrated booklet called *Europe in Figures*, published in 1988. This is an ideal publication for the general reader who wants an easily assimilated and comprehensive coverage of the Community in statistical terms. It is superbly presented and is something that the United Kingdom Statistical Office could profitably emulate.

The Community also has a first-class information service. The Information Office of the Commission of the European Communities at 8 Storey's Gate, London SW1P 3AT, provides a wide range of free material as well as subscription matter. Some is in the form of Background Reports and some are periodicals in the European Documentation series. These periodicals, of which there are a large number, cover specific topics in great detail. They are an excellent starting point from which to begin the study of a given subject. The European Parliament has its own information service at 2 Queen Anne's Gate, London SW1H 9AA. Their material too is up to date and well presented. Its monthly newspaper *European Parliament News* is rather an odd mixture of news and opinion but is worth reading for the breadth, if not the depth, of its coverage.

Since these largely free sources of up-to-date information about the Community are readily available, I have tried, in this book, to concentrate on ideas, trends and developments rather than upon creating a factual reference book. I have tried to stimulate deeper thought about the Community and the United Kingdom's present and future role in it.

This is not, as will be apparent to the reader, a neutral book. It is written from the viewpoint that, although it has its faults, the Community has major achievements to its credit and that the United Kingdom would benefit from a more wholehearted commitment to it. The Community would be better for such a commitment. The age of the nation state is on the wane; the future lies in cooperation and pooled sovereignty.

Jean Monnet, the 'father of the Community', said 'we are not forming coalitions between states, but union among people'. In other words, European integration is aimed at the hearts and minds of ordinary people. He concluded his memoirs by saying 'and the Community itself is only a stage on the way to the organised world of tomorrow.'

This great vision of Monnet, who was an extremely practical man, can only be fully appreciated against a historical background. This is why this book has a section evaluating the historical context of the progress of the Community. The Anglo-Saxon experience of modern history has been markedly different from that of the continental European. In this difference lies the explanation of our alternative views of the Community, its institutions and its future.

S. F. Goodman

Contemporary Issues 1

The European Community is at a major crossroads in its development. The decisions made in the late 1980s and the early 1990s will dictate what sort of institution will evolve. Some fear that a 'fortress Europe' will emerge, devoted to economic and political self-interest and impervious to the needs of the rest of the world. Others, mainly European socialists or social democrats, fear that a Europe fit only for capitalists will emerge. Some others are frightened of the prospect of the development of an interventionist bureaucracy trying to foist its ideas of a social market on to unwilling victims. There is an anxiety about loss of national sovereignty in key areas of decision-making. In contrast, others extol the virtues of the pooling of sovereignty. There are a few visionaries who foresee the creation of a federal state of Europe with federal institutions such as a common currency, a central bank, a European police force and eventually a European defence and foreign policy. Others, more practically, see a slow but inexorable pressure building up towards the establishment of more institutions in common. They expect to see greater uniformity of policies and the setting up of joint facilities like a European currency alongside, but not initially replacing, existing national currencies. They are willing to wait to allow the economic and political pressures involved in the realisation of a single European market to show the logical inevitability of their ideas.

Within the United Kingdom, the government under Mrs Thatcher's personal direction has begun to wage an active campaign

1

against any extension of Community powers into the social, political and economic spheres beyond those strictly necessary to implement the achievement of the single internal market. In contrast, the Labour Party has begun to reverse its traditional antagonism to the Community and has discovered new delights in the European proposals for a social market. They hope to derive all sorts of benefits from Europe that they have failed to obtain within the United Kingdom.

The Single European Act

The catalyst for change has been the Single European Act. This is referred to throughout this book and its likely effects on the Community are discussed fully in Chapter 10. In brief, the Act is an attempt to realise the original objective of the creation of the European Economic Community under the Treaty of Rome in 1957. The intention then was to have a single market without barriers of any kind between the six countries that made up the original Community. As the Community has enlarged to twelve members it became increasingly clear that many physical and technical barriers remained to prevent the free movement of goods, services and people. Internal customs barriers had gone but Europe was not a single market. As a result, in 1985, the Heads of Government of the Twelve agreed to complete the single internal market progressively by 31 December 1992. The Single European Act which implemented their agreement was signed in February 1986 and came into force on 1 July 1987. The establishment of the truly frontierless single market will involve the passing of about 300 measures. By early 1989 about two-thirds of these had already been approved. The remainder were mainly on schedule but it was becoming apparent where the main problems would arise. These areas of difficulty are in monetary policy, the harmonisation of taxation, border controls to combat terrorism and drug trafficking, and a variety of social measures. Strictly speaking, the social measures are not a direct part of the single market programme but the Commission of the Community is keen to press ahead and cater for what they call the 'social dimension' of the single market. As President Mitterrand of France has said, 'Europe will be for workers as well as for bankers.'

Decision-making in the Community

Before discussing these areas of controversy, it will help if an outline is drawn of the Community's institutions and the process of decision-making. Details of these are discussed in subsequent chapters, especially in Chapter 4.

The Community has four main institutions: the Commission, the Council, the European Parliament, and the European Court of Justice.

The Commission

This consists of seventeen members who are appointed for four years. It proposes policy and legislation. The Council discusses these proposals and the Commission will then amend or adopt them. The Commission also executes the Council's decisions and supervises the daily running of the Community. Finally, the Commission acts as the guardian of the treaties and can take legal action against members who do not comply with Community rules.

The Council

This body makes the decisions for the Community. The Council sometimes comprises meetings of ministers for a subject (Council of Ministers) or Council Working Groups made up of officials from member states. The term Council also includes the Committee of Permanent Representatives of the members (COREPER). The meetings of ministers are held each April, June and October. Twice a year the Heads of Government meet in what is called the European Council.

The European Parliament

It consists of 518 members directly elected for five years. There were elections in June 1989. Its opinion is required on many of the Commission's proposals before the Council can adopt them. It is not a legislative body in the usual sense of the word. The Parliament's activities are based in three locations. It meets in Strasbourg, but its committee meetings are in Brussels and its secretariat operates in

Luxembourg. It is making a brave, but probably fruitless, attempt to locate all its activities in Brussels.

The Court of Justice

This court has thirteen judges and six advocates-general. It rules on the interpretation and application of Community law and its judgments are binding in member states (see Chapter 8).

There are in addition to these four institutions, a Court of Auditors to audit the revenue and expenditure of the Community, an Economic and Social Committee with 156 members to advise on proposals relating to economic and social matters, and a European Investment Bank. The Economic and Social Committee has a membership of representatives of employers, trade unions and consumers.

Community Legislation

It will also be helpful to see in what forms the Community achieves its will. The Council and Commission may make regulations, issue directives, take decisions, make recommendations or deliver opinions.

Regulations

These are applicable to all member states and do not need to be approved by national parliaments. The regulation takes legal precedence if there is any conflict with national law (see Chapter 8).

Directives

These state the result that must be achieved within a stated period and it is up to each member to introduce or amend laws to bring about the desired effect. If the member fails to implement the directive the Commission may refer the matter to the Court of Justice if other approaches fail.

Decisions

These are addressed to member states, companies or individuals and are completely binding on them.

Recommendations and Opinions

These simply state the views of the institution that issues them and are not binding.

Although the legislative power of the Community lies in the Council it delegates some of its power to the Commission. This delegation is usually of routine and technical matters and is subject to the advice and assistance of committees composed of people from each member state.

Until the Single European Act decisions of the Council had to be unanimous. Since its passage decisions in some areas of policy still have to be unanimous. But one of the most significant changes to the principles of the Community has been to end an individual country's power of veto. Thus in areas directly associated with the creation of the single market it is possible to proceed with a qualified majority of 54 votes out of a total of 76. The United Kingdom, France, Germany and Italy have 10 votes each; Spain has 8; Belgium, Greece, the Netherlands and Portugal 5 each; Denmark and Ireland 3 each and Luxembourg 2.

The process of decision-making is very complex and creates a great range of opportunities for pressure groups and lobbyists. Figure 1.1 is a summary of the Community legislative process.

There is another simplified version of this flow chart in Chapter 4 where unanimity and national sovereignty are discussed. Suffice it to say, however, that such flow charts do not reveal where the power of decision actually lies. In the Community the location of final decision-making may be the Council but those decisions are based upon a long series of discussions, meetings and lobbying in Brussels and Strasbourg and in members' own corridors of power. Some commentators attribute most power to the permanent officials of the Commission, to COREPER and to those Commissioners who are active and well versed in Community power broking. In the background, there is always a tension between the national representatives working in Europe who tend to develop a wider European

FIGURE 1.1
Community Legislative Process – New Cooperation Procedure

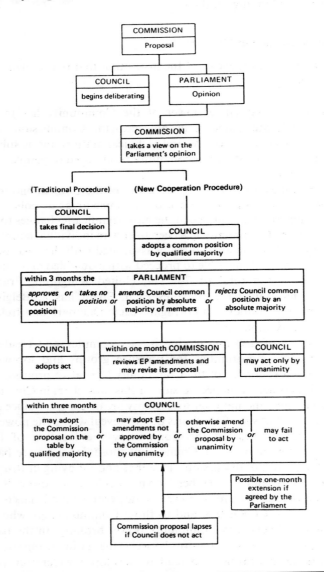

SOURCE   *The Single Market – the Facts* (London: DTI, COI).

vision, and their departments back home who tend to have a more constricted view. The truth is that the power of decision-making is shared and also shifts between and within groups according to personalities, subject matter and national perceptions of their self-interest. There is not yet the same degree of interest shown by political scientists writing in English, in the Community's power structures as there has been in national structures such as those of the United States or Britain. It is worth bearing in mind, however, the question of the process of decision-making when we return to considering the issues currently arising in the Community.

What Sort of Community Is Emerging?

A 'fortress Europe'

This may evolve as a result of the changes in progress for establishing the single internal market although this is definitely not the stated intention of the Heads of Government or Community officials. The phrase 'fortress Europe' has several interpretations and it is used, essentially, as a term of abuse. It means, in principle, that the Community will be setting up a unified market of 320 million relatively affluent people which will be able to fix an external tariff barrier to protect itself against competition from Japan, the Far East and the United States. It will also be able to exercise powerful bargaining strength against the individual nations of the world to obtain raw materials, primary products and energy at low cost. It will be able to use its establishment, or harmonisation, of standards to place external suppliers at a disadvantage (see Chapter 3: Trade Theory). In negotiations under the General Agreement on Tariffs and Trade (GATT) it could, if it chose, act in a selfish and self-centred manner. It already speaks with a unified voice at GATT talks but, until the single market is established, there are still some national divisions of interest and emphasis.

It is also possible, if the 'fortress Europe' approach came to be adopted, that the banking, monetary and financial systems might be used to discriminate against non-members. This would, of course, be easier if the Community adopted a common currency and formed a European central bank and if the United Kingdom joined the Exchange Rate Mechanism, part of the European Monetary System. Such discrimination would not find favour with the United Kingdom because of its international financial links and its free movement of foreign exchange. The United Kingdom abolished controls on foreign exchange and capital movements in 1979 and is unlikely to wish to return to even partial controls. The Labour Party has sometimes asserted that it would consider some forms of limited controls on some types of capital transfer because it dislikes the enormous outflow of funds for investment abroad. It argues that much of the money should remain in the United Kingdom and be invested in the creation of employment here. If the European Community does establish a common currency and an Exchange Rate Mechanism including sterling, it would be the most important single financial unit in world markets. (See Chapter 7 for an elaboration of this discussion.)

Another aspect of the potential 'fortress Europe' which worries some observers is that the Community might become less accessible or even inaccessible to some groups of outsiders. Within the members' boundaries there should emerge, by 1992, complete freedom of movement of citizens to work, live and set up enterprises. The fear is that the rules and regulations used to establish such mobility will be constructed in such a way as to exclude non-Community nationals. There is no doubt, on the one hand, that entry for tourism will be easier with only a single visa required for travel in all twelve states. On the other hand, however, there is great concern about the fate of those seeking asylum. The twelve ministers responsible for immigration agreed, in 1989, to the principle that a refugee will be able to apply once to enter the Community. If one country rejects him they all will. Once accepted by one country he will be accepted by all. They will also work out harmonisation procedures to deal with those seeking asylum. The ministers reaffirmed their support for the United Nations Convention on Refugees. This means that they will not return refugees to a country in which they have a well-founded expectation of persecution. The Community will, therefore, become a single entity for the purpose of seeking asylum. This, in itself, may not be cause for too much concern though a great deal depends on the detail of the harmonisation regulations. It is, however, combined with proposals to raise the fines on airlines who carry passengers without proper papers. Nor is it clear yet which countries' citizens will have to obtain visas to enter the Community. The various agencies which deal with refugees are expressing grave concern about the proposed new system. They are probably right to be concerned because the new system is almost bound to cause the entry requirements of each country to be geared up towards the toughest. Denmark opposed the proposals because it has the most lenient set of requirements for asylum seekers. The country which admits the refugee will take responsibility for him under the proposals. It is likely, therefore, that Denmark will receive a flood of applications as it appears to be a 'soft option', and will undoubtedly respond by toughening up its entry requirements. The new system will thus put an end to asylum seekers 'country hopping' in order to find one that will accept them. It is, of course, often very hard to tell the difference between genuine asylum seekers and those who simply want a better economic environment.

There have been various responses to the threat of the creation of 'fortress Europe'. One response has been from the Japanese who have increased the rate at which they have been investing in new manufacturing plants in Europe. A high proportion of their investment has been in the United Kingdom where, in 1987, they invested about £1.5 billion. In early 1989, Toyota announced the setting up of a new car assembly plant in Derbyshire. It will cost about £800 million. The United Kingdom is attractive to the Japanese because of the government's commitment to free trade, the relatively cheap labour force, the favourable tax system, improving labour relations, the absence of foreign exchange controls and the English language. There is also the very important factor of the favourable experience of the large number of already established Japanese firms. The existence of plenty of good golf courses may also be a consideration! In the long run, there is a likelihood that more investment from outside the Community will find its way to the cheaper labour countries such as Portugal.

Investment from the United States is also tending to increase and much of it is being concentrated in the United Kingdom. Large American multinationals are already established throughout Europe but the attractions of the United Kingdom include the language. It is apparent that both American and Japanese businesses are rather sceptical of the claims that there will not be a 'fortress Europe' or tougher barriers to surmount after 1992. The same anxieties are being expressed by businesses in other European countries that are not in the Community, for example Switzerland and Sweden. Companies from both nations are busy getting inside the Community by take-overs and new investment. Nestlé's purchase of Rowntree is an example.

One aspect of the threatened 'fortress' is the effect it might have on Third World countries. The Community has an assortment of programmes to help such countries and is, on the whole, generous. Through the three Lomé Conventions it has allocated large sums to helping African, Caribbean and Pacific (ACP) countries. In 1986–90, it proposes to spend 7400 million ECU under the Third Lomé Convention. It spent 4700 million on the Second between 1981 and 1985 and 3000 million on the First between 1975 and 1980. This money is paid through the European Development Fund. The details of this and other schemes are discussed in Chapter 6. The ACP countries in the Lomé Convention have free access to the Community for most of their agricultural and manufactured goods. There is a special system called Stabex to help stabilise their export earnings, and another called Sysmin to stabilise earnings from mining products. The fear is that Third World countries that are not favoured by the Lomé Conventions or by bilateral agreements will suffer from Community competition in world markets. They may also be deprived of fair competition for their goods within Europe. Some experts allege that the Community has already damaged less developed countries by subsidising exports of food and by undercutting their embryonic manufacturing industries. The Lomé Convention is undoubtedly an excellent and generous scheme. It gives aid in what seems to be a relevant, specific and well-balanced manner aimed at self-sufficiency and independence. The main concern is for those nations who are not signatories, especially Asian countries.

A free market for capitalists

The United Kingdom government was an enthusiastic supporter of the Single European Act and used its House of Commons majority, with a three line whip, to ensure its swift ratification. It seems to have been somewhat carried away by its own propaganda about its own success in sweeping away regulations, controls and bureaucracy in creating the British 'economic miracle'. It seems to have deluded itself that its simple acceptance of an updated version of Adam Smith's idea of free market forces was also intended by the other eleven members. It is, of course, possible to debate the existence and reality of the British 'economic miracle' and of the real nature of cause and effect of change. The extent, for example, of the reduction of controls and bureaucracy in the United Kingdom is usually exaggerated. The concept of an 'economic miracle' leads to what are essentially semantic arguments. The stated growth rates of the United Kingdom economy depend upon what criteria for growth are adopted and upon which base years are chosen.

The other eleven members, and particularly the original six, are in favour of the single market because they see it as a logical necessity if further economic growth and the reduction of unemployment are to be achieved. A detailed analysis of the costs of a 'non-Europe' showed that all members would benefit from extra growth, a lower rate of inflation and rising employment. They realised that the new breeze of competition would carry with it some degree of social consequence in terms of the restructuring of industry, commerce and employment. They supported the proposed controls on agricultural spending in order to leave more money available for the Social and Regional Funds of the Community. These motives have led them to expect and support proposals to add new social provisions to the Community alongside the economic changes required to create the single market.

The Single European Act permits majority decisions on measures to implement the single internal market. These include transport and environmental matters but exclude items relating to taxation, the free movement of persons and the interests of employees. It has come as a shock to some British politicians, and even apparently to some members of the government, that the Community is producing binding regulations which will affect everyday life in the United Kingdom to a marked extent. Many of these apply to the environment in areas such as the decision to enforce catalytic converters on vehicles to control exhaust emissions, or to control the quality of public water supplies. Mrs Thatcher, in early 1989, decided that her ministers were giving too much away in some areas. She appears to regard this as a threat to national sovereignty and as bureaucratic control and has, therefore, taken personal charge of supervising the outcome of departmental discussions in the Community, hoping thereby to withstand the tide of change. Inevitably, she has been likened to King Canute, although we all know that King Canute was an exceptionally able king who was teaching his sycophantic courtiers a lesson by proving that he could not stem the tide as they had suggested. The outcome will be much the same. The powers were assigned by the Single European Act and it is rather too late to be squawking about them now. There are almost daily reports of changes that will be imposed against the British government's wishes – catalytic converters, water quality controls, transport regulations for example.

The real fear of the pro free marketeers is that the single market will turn out to be overregulated, bureaucratic and protectionist. Mrs Thatcher made this plain in her famous Bruges speech in 1988. Her views were restated by Mr Lawson, at that time Chancellor of the Exchequer, in 1989. He had a vision of 'a deregulated, free market, open Europe, driven by consumer choice . . . by transferring power not to Brussels but to the people'.

The United Kingdom's opposition to proposals for the single market are strongest in the field of monetary union, sterling's membership of the Exchange Rate Mechanism, merger and competition policy, and the relaxation of border controls. In all these areas the United Kingdom government seems to think that too much regulation, harmonisation and loss of sovereignty are involved. The details are discussed in Chapters 4 and 7.

A Europe with the United Kingdom on the sidelines

There is a very real danger that the United Kingdom will be relegated to the sidelines of European decision-making unless there is a radical change of approach. This is realised by many leading members of the Conservative Party, by City opinion and political commentators. On many issues, the United Kingdom stands alone. On others, it alienates opinion by its doctrinaire intransigence. Its opposition is ineffective where majority decision-making applies. The other members are now finding ways of circumventing British opposition in areas where a majority is required. The original six, for example, have made their own 'Schengen' group agreement on removing border controls. Others may join them. There are moves afoot to push the United Kingdom out of the recalculation of the ECU in September 1989. France wants the United Kingdom to join the whole system including Exchange Rate Mechanism or to leave the monetary system completely. There are major areas arising from the 1989 Delors report on the European Monetary System that will appeal to the other eleven. They may press ahead with certain proposals and leave the United Kingdom outside.

The British government is already excluding itself, by choice, from some areas of scientific research, from the Lingua programme to teach further foreign languages in schools, and from proposals to cut cardio-vascular disease by discouraging smoking. It is also against a Community-wide pensioners' identity card to give them access to cheaper fares and facilities.

This tendency to isolationism is disliked by many in Britain and is resented by other member states (see Chapter 9). Some of the issues came to a head when Spain, as President of the Council, tried to obtain agreement on a 'Social Charter' at the early 1989 meeting of Heads of Government. Strong internal opposition to the British government's opposition to change in Europe is developing. It looks as if it will be led, in the Conservative Party, by Michael Heseltine. He undoubtedly has much support from Conservative Euro MPs and from the City and industrialists. He will also receive support from trade unions who hope to benefit from the 'Social Charter'.

Conclusion

It is very unlikely that the United Kingdom will remain for long on the sidelines of Europe. Our financial and commercial self-interest dictates that we should be closely involved in change and remain in step with major competitors such as France and Germany. There will probably not be a 'fortress Europe' unless there is a major international recession. Nor will there be a 'market for bankers and not workers'. The likelihood is that there will be a free single internal market, sensibly regulated and with a strong 'Social Charter' to maintain the rights of workers and consumers, pensioners, women and minorities. There will probably be a more effective European Parliament and greater democratic participation. People will come to regard national sovereignty as pooled rather than sacrificed.

Ideas into Institutions – How the European Community Began

Many of those who witnessed the appalling slaughter and destruction of the First World War realised that only some form of unification of the states of Europe could prevent further conflict. The Great Powers' struggle of the nineteenth century, the competition for empire and the arms race had culminated in a great cataclysm. Yet the nineteenth century had shown, in the case of the unification of Germany and Italy, that wars could be reduced by political and economic union. Further afield, the success of the American federal system, despite the supreme test of the Civil War, gave hope to the European democrat. The immediate aftermath of the First World War saw the creation of several new nation states and the resurrection of old states as the Austro-Hungarian empire collapsed and the Baltic states achieved temporary independence. Many boundaries were redrawn or established and we know, with the benefit of hindsight, that the Treaty of Versailles in 1919 contained the seeds of the Second World War. Perceptive critics of the time recognised that fact. The years 1919–39 can be regarded as an extended armistice.

It was against this background that the League of Nations was formed. It is fashionable to scoff cynically at the naïvety of those who thought that the League would ensure that the Great War would be 'the war to end all wars'. Admittedly, the League got off to a very bad start when the American President, Woodrow Wilson, one of its chief architects, failed to get the endorsement of the American people for his policies at Versailles and for the League.

Yet millions saw in it a great hope for the future. The League did have some achievements. Disarmament agreements were reached. Naval building programmes were curtailed. Millions joined the Peace Pledge Union or its equivalent in other countries. The fact that these people's hopes were destroyed by the demonic forces of national socialism and deranged nationalism is for the whole of mankind to regret.

It was within this context of post First World War reconstruction that a Pan-European Movement was launched in the 1920s. It called, in 1923, for a United States of Europe based mainly on the model of the United States. A few years later, in 1929, the League of Nations' Assembly in Geneva was the forum for an attempt to form a European Union within the context of the League of Nations. This was proposed by the French and German foreign ministers. The objective was very limited. It was to leave the separate states fully sovereign but would promote closer cooperation. The great depression in industry, commerce and finance which followed prevented this scheme from being adopted. The slump also created a breeding ground for the extension of versions of fascism from Italy to Germany and the Far East. Hopes for European unity were lost until after the Second World War.

The United Kingdom and Early Ideas for European Unity

The United Kingdom and Commonwealth had suffered a great loss of life during the First World War. The United Kingdom also lost its economic pre-eminence in several fields to the United States and new producers had sprung up, especially in the Far East. Despite this, Britain had not suffered the extensive physical war damage of France, Belgium, Northern Italy, and parts of Germany. There was not the same imperative for the British to seek European unity. Britain could still find comfort in the Victorian and Edwardian visions of Empire. Although the war had enabled the independent Dominions to reach maturity, the emotional ties of imperial grandeur lingered. They persisted until it became blatantly obvious, with the independence of India, Pakistan, and Ceylon and then the flight from colonialisation in Africa after 1957, that Britain's future no longer lay outside, but within, Europe. The transition from imperial power to becoming a partner in a European Community was to prove slow, painful, and erratic. Some would say that it has not yet been achieved in the hearts of many British people.

The New Ideas After 1945

As the tide of war turned in the Allies' favour after 1943 they began to plan for the peace. Many lessons had been learned from the aftermath of the First World War. The need to have carefully worked out schemes to deal with the inevitable post-war chaos was fully understood. There was also a strong determination to try to avoid the perceived causes of the Second World War – namely, cyclical unemployment, protectionism, poverty and deprivation. These, and other similar factors, were seen as a breeding ground for fascism. There was also a fear in some quarters that post-war dislocation of society would enable communism to flourish. In Britain, this planning for the post-war years included the Beveridge Report 'Full Employment in a Free Society'. This was published in November 1944 but several parts of it had received a public airing beforehand and the government had issued its White Paper on Full Employment before Beveridge's work itself was formally published. Another great factor in post-war social change was the so-called Butler Education Act of 1944 which extended secondary education to all and opened up the higher education sector to large numbers of less well-off people. Another was the Barlow Royal Commission Report of 1941 which was reprinted in 1943 and which dealt with industrial location and population trends.

On the international scene there was a great proliferation of new institutions which applied either on a world-wide scale or on a regional basis. The major world-wide schemes which have had a profound effect on European development were the International Monetary Fund (IMF) and the International Bank for Reconstruction and Development (IBRD), usually called 'the World Bank'. With modifications these have survived to make a major contribution to international economic stability and cooperation. Another body of great long-term importance has been the Organisation for Economic Cooperation and Development (OECD). This was originally the Organisation for European Economic Cooperation (OEEC). Initially, the defeated powers, Germany and Japan, were excluded but were incorporated once their industrial and political potential was required as a pillar of American anti-communism. West Germany was resurrected into full ally status after NATO was formed as a response to the blockade of Berlin by the USSR. Japan was 'recreated' when its geographical position made it vital as a base for United Nations' operations during the Korean War of 1950–3. Meanwhile, in Eastern Europe, the previously independent nations became communist by fair and foul means and were eventually welded into an economic trading bloc with the formation of Comecon in 1949.

In Western Europe, a bewildering variety of organisations was created. Out of some of these eventually emerged the European Economic Community (EEC) or the European Community (EC) as it is now generally known.

The New Organisations

Three broad types of organisation were created. The United States and Canada had been deeply involved in the European war and in reconstruction afterwards. It was natural, therefore, that the first type had North American involvement.

The Organisation for European Economic Cooperation

In 1948, the USA sponsored the formation of the OEEC. This organisation made possible the successful implementation of the Marshall Plan. This plan, named after the American Secretary of State, provided immense amounts of financial aid in return for European cooperation in reconstruction. The sum of $17 billion was spent in the four years of the plan's operation from 1948 to 1952. It was this scheme that enabled West Germany, Italy, France and the Benelux countries to modernise their industry, to provide employment, and to create political stability in the democratic mould. The United Kingdom, which benefited only marginally or indirectly from the Marshall Plan, was left largely to its own devices. The United Kingdom, mainly from its own resources, had to reconstruct war-ravaged capital goods industries, its transport system and its housing. As a matter of what can be regarded as misplaced honour, the government committed itself to repaying its debts to the United

States, thus adding a further burden to the nation. As a partial consequence of this, and of the problems of reconstruction, a large additional loan had to be obtained from the USA. As that was spent, the pound had to be devalued in 1949. It is from this period that some of the seeds of Britain's poor post-war economic performance relative to other European nations dates. It can be argued that the United Kingdom concentrated on social reforms, on the creation of educational and health systems, on redistribution of wealth, and on social justice at the expense of reconstructing our obsolescent industrial structures. In the long run, there has proved to be little truth in the saying that the spoils of war go to the victor.

The OEEC was formed after an attempt in 1947 by France, the USSR and the United Kingdom to reach an agreement on a European recovery plan failed because of Soviet objections to the impairment of national sovereignty. France and the United Kingdom then invited all European countries except Spain (which was still a fascist dictatorship) to a conference. The list of those who accepted and took part is interesting in the light of later developments. They were Austria, Belgium, Denmark, Eire, Greece, Iceland, Italy, Luxembourg, the Netherlands, Norway, Portugal, Sweden, Switzerland, and Turkey. (Czechoslovakia initially accepted but withdrew into the Soviet bloc.) These fourteen countries, plus the United Kingdom and France, signed a convention in 1948. The zones of Germany occupied by the British, the French and the Americans were also signatories, as was the Anglo-American zone of Trieste.

The initial requirement for the OEEC was to solve the problem of Europe's enormous trade deficit with the USA, to promote maximum cooperation among the sixteen nations, to establish internal financial stability and to maximise production. In order to achieve this a Council, a Secretariat, an executive committee and several *ad hoc* committees were established. There was a very great incentive to make the system work because American aid under the Marshall Plan (European Recovery Programme) was contingent upon intra-European cooperation. It is generally agreed that the OEEC was very successful, so much so that an American administrator of Marshall Aid, Hoffman, called on the nations of the organisation to create a Western Union, a permanent free trading area of 270 million people when the European Recovery Programme ended. This has not yet fully materialised because the countries of Europe diverged for a time into different economic groupings, the EEC and EFTA (European Free Trade Association).

In 1961, the OEEC was transformed by a change of membership and by new objectives. It was renamed the Organisation for Economic Cooperation and Development (OECD). Its membership broadened to include the USA, Canada, Finland, Spain, West Germany, and Japan. The organisation has a Council on which each country is represented, and a secretary-general with a permanent staff. Its fundamental purpose is 'to achieve the highest sustainable economic growth and employment and a rising standard of living in member countries, whilst maintaining financial stability, and thus contribute to the development of the world economy'. The intention was to achieve this by freeing international trade and movements of capital. New ground was broken by the additional aim of coordinating economic aid to less developed countries (LDCs). The organisation is consultative and its decisions are not binding on its members.

The North Atlantic Treaty Organisation

NATO too was sponsored by the USA. It was formed in 1949 to create a counterweight to the military strength of the USSR and its allies. In the first phase NATO was dominated by the USA which provided huge financial and military assistance. West Germany's membership in 1955 began a new phase and the balance of power within NATO shifted more towards Europe. The period until 1967 saw the adoption of nuclear policies and the relative relegation of conventional arms into second place. This was partly a response to manpower problems but was also due to the economic and political cost of any attempt to possess both full-scale conventional and nuclear forces. Since the late 1960s France has withdrawn to the sidelines of NATO. Other countries such as Spain and Greece have reviewed their positions in relation to American bases and there have been major squabbles about the sharing of costs on an equitable basis. There has been a trend towards the USA negotiating directly with the USSR over the heads of her NATO allies.

In terms of our subject, the European Community, NATO is of importance in several ways. First, its existence should prevent any future European war because the military commands of the nations, their equipment and logistics are so interdependent. Secondly, the accumulated expenditure, capital investment, and annual expenditure on arms and defence related research are so enormous that they have a profound effect on industrial and scientific development, location of industry, communications and employment. Although the standardisation of equipment still leaves a lot to be desired, NATO purchasing exerts a great influence. A successful order for NATO equipment enables economies of scale to be achieved in manufacture and reduces costs and prices in the international market. Thirdly, the existence of NATO, with its transatlantic component of the USA and Canada and its non-European Community membership of Norway and Turkey, can be regarded as a major obstacle to the permanent, closer political unity of Europe. Its presence makes a common foreign policy harder to achieve, especially because of different national attitudes to nuclear weapons. Some would disagree and assert that NATO should make political unity easier because it has created a mechanism for systematic cooperation and consultation. In any event, there is yet another organisation which is intended to achieve greater unity.

The Brussels Pact and Western European Union

At the end of 1947 a Four Power Conference on the future of Germany failed to reach agreement. The division of Germany became inevitable. In early 1948, therefore, the British Foreign Secretary, Ernest Bevin, put forward the idea of a 'Western Union'. The Russian *coup d'état* in Czechoslovakia, overthrowing the democratic government, hastened the signing of the Treaty of Brussels, in March 1948, between the United Kingdom, France, Belgium, the Netherlands, and Luxembourg. These countries agreed to support each other militarily and to cooperate in economic matters. They set up a permanent consultative council in London. In 1949, they set up the Council of Europe which has a ministerial committee that meets in private, and a consultative body that meets in public. Under the Treaty of Brussels a defence establishment was set up at Fontainebleau under the command of Field Marshal Montgomery. He became very frustrated whilst in that job because of the vacillation of the politicians and the rigid nationalist aspirations of the French. He felt that little was achieved in terms of effective military organisation. The formation of NATO in 1949 overshadowed this aspect of the Brussels Pact.

In May 1955, the Brussels Treaty was extended to include West

Germany and Italy and create the Western European Union. (Portugal has since joined.) This modification of the treaty took the form of a fifty-year Western European Unity Treaty and the formation of the Western European Union. This resulted from an idea, born in 1948 at The Hague Conference, to form a supranational European army. The plan was conceived by the French Prime Minister, René Pleven, and later put forward to the Council of Europe in 1951 by Robert Schumann, the French Foreign Minister. It was intended to make German rearmament acceptable. It would also make progress towards a federal Europe easier. This idea of a European Defence Community was supported by the USA but opinion in France, Italy and Scandinavia was very divided. A preliminary treaty was concluded but gradually East–West tension decreased. De Gaulle was strongly opposed to the plan because he favoured a confederation of sovereign European states with France in the ascendancy. He wanted Europe to be independent of American dominance. The plan for a European Defence Community failed because the United Kingdom would not cooperate as a result of its commitment to the defence of its remaining empire. There was no further discussion on the political union of Europe until 1961. The British government under Churchill and Eden refused to sacrifice British independence to a European integration of forces. The French Assembly rejected the European Defence Community in 1954 and the United Kingdom proposed a compromise in the form of a high level of cooperation between the national armies. This was to be controlled by the Council of the Brussels Treaty. As a result the Western European Unity Treaty was signed and the Western European Union established. It was under this treaty that West Germany agreed not to attempt any changes to its borders by force, and not to make nuclear, chemical or biological weapons. It also agreed not to make large naval vessels, long-range bombers or long-range missiles.

In practice, as has already been said, the major military cooperation in Europe is through NATO rather than through the Western European Union. Although the cooperation on defence matters has been largely carried out by NATO, the WEU has, since 1984, become a vehicle for establishing a stronger European voice in the defence of Europe as against American influence. France, which became a peripheral member of NATO under President de Gaulle, has instigated a revival of the WEU. This has been significant as the

USA and USSR have taken increasingly to direct negotiations with each other on armaments, as in the Geneva Treaty of 1988.

The Council of Europe

European nations differ greatly in the degree to which they are able or willing to sacrifice or subordinate their sovereignty to international or supranational bodies. Sweden and Switzerland have a long history of neutrality. Austria has neutrality forced upon it by the treaty re-establishing it as an independent state. It has also come to value neutrality. Others, such as France and the United Kingdom are very reluctant to cede sovereignty. There is, therefore, a place for an organisation which enables states to belong without commitment to ideas of political union, federal or confederate. The Council of Europe is just such an organisation. It was established in May 1949 by ten nations (United Kingdom, France, Benelux, Italy, Ireland, Denmark, Norway and Sweden). The number has been increased to twenty-one by the addition of Austria, West Germany, Cyprus, Switzerland, Portugal, Spain, Greece, Turkey, Iceland, Malta and Liechtenstein. The Council of Europe is an important means through which nations cooperate. Superficially, its constitution looks unpromising. Its decisions are made by a Committee of Ministers and they must be unanimous. In practice, therefore, each nation can operate a veto. There is a consultative body called a Parliamentary Assembly. It cannot pass legislation but simply makes recommendations to the Committee of Ministers. After they have agreed a proposal it still has to be ratified by the parliaments of each nation. Despite this inauspicious arrangement the Council of Europe has produced many agreements in legal, social, cultural and economic spheres. Most noteworthy is the European Convention for the Protection of Human Rights and Fundamental Freedoms which was adopted in 1950. This convention set up the European Court of Human Rights and the European Commission for Human Rights.

The Economic Organisations

The day to day working of the Organisation of European Economic Cooperation after 1948 in putting the European Recovery Programme (Marshall Plan) into effect forced the nations of Europe into economic and financial cooperation. As the Marshall Plan was scheduled to end in 1952 there was pressure to create a permanent economic organisation. It is from this area that the European Community as we know it came into being. The Community is technically and legally three organisations operating together. These are the European Coal and Steel Community (ECSC), the European Atomic Energy Community (Euratom) and the European Economic Community (EEC).

When these three bodies and their development are studied it is apparent that they have created a unique structure. They have not adopted either of the two major suggestions for a unified Europe that have been put forward over the years – that is the federal and the confederate solutions. A federal system is one where states form a political unity while remaining independent as to their internal affairs. This sounds a simple concept but the main problem, and area of future dispute, is the degree of decision-making given to the central government. The central government always manages defence and foreign policy but there remain 'grey' areas of disputed jurisdiction which emerge over time. The written constitution of such federal states usually includes a statement about 'residual' powers and who is to possess them. This is frequently the central government. Two classic cases are nuclear energy and air transport regulation in the USA. The founding fathers of the American constitution could not predict either. Such conflicts make the existence of an arbitrating body essential, as in the US Supreme Court. None of the suggestions for a federal state of Europe has made progress despite the relative success of the federal system in West Germany, the USA, Canada and Australia. One of the most interesting speculations about the future of the Community is whether there will be a stronger trend towards a more federal approach, that is a Community foreign policy and defence policy. There are signs of this emerging with an attempt at a joint policy on South Africa. There is also an attempt to create a more independent European defence posture in the light of the long-term possibility that the USA may gradually withdraw from European defence except for the provision of a 'nuclear umbrella'.

A confederation is an alliance or league of states who retain their independence and who make decisions by consultation. Although central administration and decision-making bodies have to be set up, the emphasis is on the sovereignty of the separate states.

Confederacies tend to be weak and relapse into separatism and acrimony in times of stress. Some of the European organisations already discussed are essentially confederal in nature.

The unique structure of the Community lies in the fact that the twelve members have adopted what is generally called 'integration' as a policy. They have ceded parts of their national sovereignty to the Community and given it some sovereign powers which it can exercise. These powers, in certain circumstances, have the force of national law. The objective is to create a permanent and indissoluble organisation and political entity. It should be remembered that a major motive in the steps towards European unity was the removal of any future possibility of the re-emergence of an expansionist, militarily strong, Germany. The way to prevent this was to bind Germany inextricably into an economic web and into a mutual defence organisation. The USSR, whilst not wholly in favour of a rich, economically powerful West Germany, was happier that no independent West German military power could be envisaged. It does, however, retain a strong vested interest in a divided Germany.

The first economic institution – the European Coal and Steel Community

The ECSC was formed by a treaty signed, in April 1951, by Belgium, France, Germany, Italy, Luxembourg and the Netherlands. It came into force in July 1952. It originated in a plan put forward in May 1950 by Robert Schumann, the French foreign minister. He and Jean Monnet proposed that French and German coal and steel production should be put under a joint authority in an organisation which other countries could join. Some see this plan as stemming from a typically Churchillian proposal at Zurich in 1946 when he called for a United States of Europe in order to create Franco-German cooperation. Needless to say, he did not see the United Kingdom as a member of such a United States because of Britain's imperial, world status, but merely as a sort of benevolent promoter.

After the formation of the ECSC there followed a period of political manoeuvring to ensure that a rearmed Germany could be contained. German rearmament had become essential for political and manpower reasons after the Berlin blockade by the USSR in 1948–9. NATO had been formed and the Warsaw pact signed. The so-called Iron Curtain dividing East and West had fully descended and the 'Cold War' had begun in earnest. As mentioned above, one attempt to solve Europe's defence problems was the European Defence Community (treaty 1951) which would have created a supranational European defence force. Britain refused to join in and the French Assembly rejected the plan in 1954. As a result a new way forward had to be found. This took the form of an initiative by the ECSC foreign ministers in 1955. Their experience of working through ECSC indicated that a united Europe could be created. They met at a conference at Messina and set up a committee under Paul Spaak, the Belgian foreign minister, to study possibilities for further integration. The committee reported in 1956. A series of negotiations followed and two treaties were signed at Rome on 25 March 1957. These established the European Economic Community (EEC) and the European Atomic Community (Euratom). They took effect on 1 January 1958.

The British responded by a proposal to set up a European Free Trade Association (which became known as EFTA). This had the great benefit of involving no loss of national sovereignty and was, therefore, more attractive to those members of both the Conservative Party who were in government and of the Labour Party in opposition, who were strongly antagonistic towards any transfer of parliamentary powers to a European body. The details of the British reaction to European unification are dealt with in the next chapter.

We have seen the long, involved and uncertain progress of ideas into real organisations from the early 1920s to 1956. To understand the process fully we need to try to see it from the point of view of a continental European trying to prevent yet another devastating power struggle from following two world wars. This gives a completely different perspective from that of the Briton who tends only to see loss of sovereignty, budget problems and food surpluses when looking at the European Community. In terms of its political objective of securing peace and cooperation between France and Germany, the Community has been an outstanding success.

DATE CHART

1923–29   Pan-European movement within the League of Nations. It proposed a federal states of Europe. It failed with the onset of the depression.

1948–52   European Recovery Programme (Marshall Plan). This pumped American money into the reconstruction of Europe.

1948   The Organisation for European Economic Cooperation was formed to make the Marshall Plan effective. Sixteen countries joined initially: Austria, Belgium, Denmark, Eire, France, Greece, Iceland, Italy, Luxembourg, Netherlands, Norway, Portugal, Sweden, Switzerland, Turkey, and the UK. It also included the zones of Germany occupied by Britain, France and the USA. In 1961 it was renamed the Organisation for Economic Cooperation and Development and extended to include the USA, Canada, Finland, Spain, West Germany, and Japan.

1949   The North Atlantic Treaty Organisation (NATO) was instituted in April by twelve nations: USA, UK, Luxembourg, Canada, France, Netherlands, Belgium, Norway, Italy, Denmark, Portugal and Iceland. West Germany joined in 1955.

1948   Brussels Treaty signed in March by UK, France, Belgium, Netherlands and Luxembourg to create military and economic cooperation. It led to:

1949   The Council of Europe (May 1949). This originally consisted of ten nations, UK, France, Belgium, Netherlands, Luxembourg, Ireland, Italy, Denmark, Norway and Sweden. (In 1988 it consists of twenty-one nations.) It, in turn, led to:

1950   The European Convention for the Protection of Human Rights and Fundamental Freedoms which led to the setting up of the Court of Human Rights and the Commission for Human Rights.

1951   European Defence Community Treaty. This failed to set up a supranational European army.

1955   Western European Union set up in May by UK, France, Belgium, Netherlands and Luxembourg, the signatories of the Brussels Treaty of 1948, plus West Germany and Italy. Portugal has since joined. It was a compromise suggested by the UK after the 1951 European Defence Community Treaty failed in 1954.

1951   The European Coal and Steel Community Treaty was signed in April by Belgium, Netherlands, Luxembourg, France, Italy and West Germany. It came into force in July 1952.

1957   The Treaties of Rome were signed on 25 March by the 'Six', Belgium, France, West Germany, Netherlands, Luxembourg and Italy creating Euratom and the European Economic Community. They came into force on 1 January 1958.

Why Did the United Kingdom Join?

The Six

The Six set themselves economic and political targets. People in the United Kingdom viewed these at first with scepticism and then with trepidation as they were achieved or surpassed. Some of the targets had a time-scale attached. The first major objective, without which the others could not be achieved, was to form a customs union. There was a wide diversity of customs tariffs on imports into and between the six countries. They tended to be low into Germany and the Benelux countries and high into Italy and France. The Six aimed at abolishing these differences within twelve years from 1958. They wanted all duties on the movement of goods within the Community abolished. They would then set up a common customs tariff (a CCT) on goods entering the Six from abroad. They achieved this ahead of schedule. In 1968, customs duties within the six states were abolished. They then established a common external tariff on all goods entering the Community from non-member states. As the stages towards the successful accomplishment of this target were completed the United Kingdom became more keenly aware that it would eventually be forced into a very uncompetitive position in its major European markets. The United Kingdom's goods would have to overcome the CCT. Meanwhile, the European producers would have the benefits of the greater economies of scale derived from their larger home markets. These would give them lower average costs of production within Europe, in the United Kingdom and in world markets.

What Are the Economics of the Community as a Customs Union?

The European Community is a classic example of a customs union. The members agree to remove customs or tariff barriers between them and to impose a common external tariff on imports from non-member countries. This external tariff can be used as a protectionist hurdle by being set at a level that places the imports at a cost disadvantage. It can be made more favourable to friendly nations. Such an action has tended to provoke retaliation and bilateral or preferential trading agreements. The General Agreement on Tariffs and Trade (GATT) was set up to reverse the 1930s' trend which had seen the world sink into a desperate round of protection and 'beggar my neighbour' policies. The Community has been an important participant in GATT and in the regular 'rounds' of discussions that try to improve its application and effectiveness. Two rounds, the Kennedy and Tokyo rounds, have been completed and a third, the Uruguay round, is currently, in 1989, at an interim stage.

Despite its members being signatories of the GATT agreements, and despite the participation of the Community as a single entity in the successive rounds, the European Community has frequently come into conflict with other nations about its trading policy. The Community has gradually removed its less acceptable practices in relation to the Third World in a series of negotiations ending in the 1975 Lomé Convention. The convention is regularly updated and the Third Agreement was signed in 1984. The conventions are mainly concerned with aid but also relate to trade. Some critics think that there is a cosmetic element in the conventions to cover up the real harm that they allege stems from Community trading policies, especially the subsidising of exports from the Twelve.

One of the most constructive and promising developments from the Lomé Conventions is a fund called Stabex. This is used to stabilise the earnings of the sixty African, Caribbean and Pacific (ACP) countries in the agreement. It applies to fifty agricultural commodities. Stabex is an insurance fund financed largely from the European Development Fund and augmented by payments from the

ACP countries when their export earnings exceed certain levels. This principle has also been extended to mining products with a fund called Sysmin.

Whilst Third World opposition to the European Community has become muted there has been growing criticism from the United States. Japan too has voiced its concern. The United States has traditionally been a fairly protectionist country, some say excessively so. The nature of the United States Congress means that each Senator and Representative must fight for his own state or district and its industries. As a result the United States has a formidable set of quota and tariff barriers together with a maze of administrative and health regulations. They all tend to restrict imports. In recent years, therefore, it has been inevitable that major clashes should have occurred between the United States and the Community. The main areas of dispute have been steel products, agricultural goods and textiles. Other products may be drawn in to the fray as part of retaliatory measures. It is usually the United States that is alleging 'unfair' competition. From its point of view the European Community protects its own markets and sometimes subsidises exports. Most of these disputes are eventually resolved peacefully. Another area of dispute is the United States' attempts to control the export and re-export of certain high technology products such as computers and electronic systems to the Soviet bloc. This is seen by many European companies as a gross interference with their commercial freedoms.

The main theoretical objection to customs unions such as the European Community is expressed in the so-called Law of Comparative Cost Advantage. This theory concludes that free trade maximises the use of the world's resources and that any interference, such as tariffs or quotas, with the free movement of goods and services reduces mankind's economic satisfaction. It states that a country will tend to specialise in, and export, those goods in which it has the greatest comparative cost advantage in production, or, in which it has the least comparative cost disadvantage. It should be emphasised that trade benefits both the most and the least favoured nation if their comparative costs of production differ. This applies even if one country is superior, in cost terms, at producing everything. These comparative costs and the terms of trade can explain which goods a country exports and which it imports. Most economics textbooks contain a numerical example to illustrate the principle of comparative cost advantage. The theory is a specific application of Adam Smith's demonstration of the gains to be had from the division of labour and specialisation. The theory tends to rely too heavily on the idea of the factors of production, land, labour and capital, being more mobile within each country than they actually are. It also tends to gloss over problems related to transport costs, economies of scale and different currencies. Having said that, it is still generally accepted that free trade is an ideal that should be aspired to by all nations.

The European Community's external tariffs are a clear breach of the ideal of free trade and so are the various methods used by individual members to restrict imports. Unfortunately, it is always possible for nations to ignore the economic imperative of the theory of comparative cost advantage and to argue in favour of protectionism for strategic reasons. They also sometimes claim that foreign countries are 'dumping' goods on them. This is a complex field but means that the seller is selling at a price below the average cost of production. This is certainly done with some Soviet bloc products. It is also alleged that it is done for gains in short-term market share with some Japanese products. Needless to say, it has been alleged by the USA that the European Community has also 'dumped' agricultural products and some types of steel. The GATT is intended to help prevent and stop dumping.

Have the United Kingdom's Hopes Been Met?

There is no doubt that those who believed the optimists who predicted enormous gains from trade for the United Kingdom when it joined the Community, have been sadly disappointed. The major gains have apparently been to continental firms who have exploited the United Kingdom market. This is not too surprising since they were already obtaining some of the benefits of a larger market. It could be argued also that British industry and commerce was too complacent, too sheltered and too much in the grip of slack management and overpowerful trade unions. Moreover, few could have predicted the powerful expansion of the Japanese into British, European and world markets. They, of course, achieved this success through very thorough planning, marketing skills and a very close partnership between government, civil service, business leaders and trade unions.

Gradually, the United Kingdom has begun to exploit and benefit from the larger European market. Lessons have been learned, firms have become more efficient and competitive. Many large British firms are developing into market leaders in Europe and are assuming a more multinational aspect. It is stated that the removal of barriers to trade by 1992 presents a great challenge to businesses. This is a statement of the obvious. What is less accepted is that it also represents an enormous challenge to government to ensure that the right infrastructure is in place in time. This requires first-class transport and communications systems. There is little sign that this need has been recognised and there is every possibility that British industry will not be able to benefit fully from the greater freedom of the single market and its potential economies of scale. The United Kingdom may end up as a peripheral backwater economically unless the means of moving goods cheaply, quickly and competitively are provided. The other members of the Community see this as a role for government. They have been proved right in the past. Experience suggests that the United Kingdom government will realise too late and will react with inadequate resources. If you doubt this statement consider the delays on the Thames barrage, the M4, the M25 and the piecemeal railway electrification to Scotland. It is safe to predict that by the year 2000 there will be many books discussing the vexed question of what happened to the North Sea oil revenues. They could have been used to create an infrastructure suitable for the single European market.

Economies of Scale – the Great Sales Pitch?

The concept of economies of scale needs to be understood if the motivation for creating the Community, and for the United Kingdom's desire to join, are to be appreciated. 'Economies of scale' was a phrase very much in vogue in the 1960s and was used to justify many mergers, take-overs and nationalisation schemes. The proponents of such schemes conveniently forgot that there are *diseconomies* of scale, particularly in management, and that a high level of demand needs to exist to enable large plants to produce at their most efficient or lowest cost per unit. For example, a steel plant designed to produce 3 million tonnes of steel per year only has cost advantages derived from large-scale output if it is actually producing its designed output. If it is producing only 1 million tonnes as a result of depressed demand, it may have average costs per tonne which are higher than a smaller plant which *is* producing at *its* designed optimum. Large plants have larger capital costs in terms of interest charges and depreciation. These need to be spread over a greater volume of output. 'Economies of scale' is still a popular phrase in the 1980s, despite a great deal of evidence to indicate that 'medium'-sized firms are frequently more efficient and profitable than 'large' firms.

An economy of large-scale production simply means that the average cost of production per unit of output falls as the level of output produced by additional inputs of all factors of production together is increased. The costs may fall because of technical factors derived from the size of plant and equipment. For example, a 200 000 tonne oil tanker does not cost twice as much to build and operate as two 100 000 tonne tankers. A larger internal market, such as the Six, or the present Twelve, obviously increases the potential for obtaining technical economies of scale. There is, however, a risk of diseconomies arising from having inflexible levels of output. This occurred with steel production where too many extremely large plants were built at a time when the demand was dropping. This happened because of recession and the growth of demand for substitutes for steel. These substitutes are mainly plastics and aluminium alloys, or, in the case of office machinery or cash registers, electronic chips.

The other two main types of economy of scale which were most relevant to those viewing the early development of the EEC were those normally called 'commercial' economies and 'marketing' economies. Commercial economies refer to those reductions in costs derived from being able to buy raw materials and components in bulk at cheaper prices per unit. These apply most obviously in the types of large-scale retailing pioneered by Tesco, Sainsbury, and Marks and Spencer. They also apply to large-scale manufacturers of domestic consumer durable goods such as cars and white goods. 'Marketing economies', which have been used to justify all sorts of mergers between firms producing unconnected products, derive from reductions in costs per unit in the selling, distribution and advertising of products and services. Certain volumes of sales are usually necessary before national advertising, particularly on television, is worthwhile. These economies partly explain the trend towards 'product ranges', company 'logos', company own brands and international firms, or multinationals. Economists and entrepreneurs saw endless scope for these types of economies of scale within the Six, particularly as the growth of incomes and demand was very high. The pursuit of economies of scale went hand in hand with attempts to spread the risks of enterprise. This partly explains the growth of conglomerates and diversifying mergers in the 1970s and 1980s although the late 1980s saw a contrary trend towards the break-up of some conglomerates.

There are other types of economies of scale in the usual classifications. In one of these, 'financial economies', many people in the United Kingdom felt that they had a great deal to teach the Europeans. This sense of superiority, which has turned out to be largely unfounded, was based upon the different historical experience of the United Kingdom and most European countries in the financial crash of 1931 and the great depression generally. It was also based upon the then dominant international role of the City of London in world financial and capital markets, and sterling in the 'sterling area'. This dominance in the 1950s (except over New York) has disappeared as the relative isolation of markets has vanished with the advent of advanced telecommunications. It has also succumbed to the effects of stronger economic growth in Japan and West Germany. Moreover, the supposed superiority of the United Kingdom banking system over the continental system is now regarded as a source of relative weakness. In the 1930s, continental banks suffered very badly because they were directly concerned with the ownership of shares in large, and small, companies. Their fortunes were entwined and, as the depression bit deeply, the companies collapsed and brought down the banks. In the United Kingdom, the system of branch banking and the avoidance of direct investment in company equities enabled United Kingdom banks to survive. They preferred purchases of government stock (gilt-edged investment) and secured loans to industry, to the purchase of stock in companies. This tradition has persisted and some people regard it as a major cause of the alleged failure of the City of London to provide risk capital to British entrepreneurs. The continental system encourages a longer term view of the return on capital than the

British which tends towards an extremely short-run view.

It was, therefore, the 'holy grail' of economies of scale which acted as a major lure to British businessmen and politicians in the early 1960s, as they saw the Six successfully building their customs unions and achieving faster economic growth than the United Kingdom.

The economic case for the United Kingdom joining the EEC was strongly based on the idea that British industry could compete effectively against continental firms in the larger market, especially with the backing of a large overseas market as well. It was also thought, though not as frequently expressed, that the new competition would give British industry a much needed jolt and force it to adopt a more cost-conscious and consumer-oriented approach. (There were grave doubts about the effects on United Kingdom agriculture. These will be discussed in Chapter 5.) The economic case for entry seemed strong, although some prescient folk realised that the United Kingdom might suffer in its internal markets from fierce competition from some already more efficient continental producers. These doubters' fears were borne out in the 1970s and 1980s in the case, for example, of motor vehicle manufacture. Some long-sighted folk worried that the United Kingdom might become a mere periphery of an industrial and commercial economic core centred between France and Germany and spilling over into Belgium and Holland. It was rather like the effects of completing the M1 motorway between London and Leeds. Some optimists thought that it would enable northern based firms to get out of their localised markets and sell to the South. Generally, the reverse has happened. The larger market concentrations of the South and southern Midlands have tended to cause a drift of enterprise to these areas. The 'North' is now supplied from larger plants in the South which benefit more from economies of scale derived from proximity to a large market. Improvements in road transport, containerisation, specialised vehicles, refrigerated lorries and higher average speeds and loads, favour the drift to location in larger markets. 'Larger' here means in terms of numbers of people and in terms of average incomes per head.

The economic case was gradually accepted, although many thought a similar case could be made for staying with the European Free Trade Association (EFTA) and the Commonwealth and the North Atlantic link. There was, however, also a major change in political attitudes in the 1950s and 1960s.

Changing Political Attitudes in the United Kingdom

The emphasis of victory over Germany and Japan in 1945 after six weary years of war disguised for a time the reality of the United Kingdom's position in global politics. Politicians of all complexions were slow to grasp the new conditions of world dominance by the USA and USSR. For a time all efforts were concentrated on the reconstruction of a distorted and investment starved industrial structure from war production to peaceful applications. Demobilisation and redistribution of labour were at the forefront of everyone's minds. Rationing intensified despite the peace, and a fuel shortage persisted. Power cuts were an accepted winter occurrence until the early 1960s as demand outstripped supply. Efforts were made by all the colonial powers, including the United Kingdom, to restore their pre-war colonial possessions. From these efforts, which were only temporarily successful, stemmed the Vietnam War and the Algerian conflicts as the French colonial yoke was resisted. Britain, for its part, faced a succession of colonial struggles, all of which ended in independence for the colony.

The writing was on the wall when the Labour government granted Indian independence in 1947. It was impossible to stem the tide of Indian nationalism any longer. It had only been held in check by the exigencies of war. The partition into India, Pakistan and Ceylon was forced upon a reluctant British government. The subsequent violence and mass murder during the period of transfer of government seemed, initially, to justify the fierce critics of the granting of independence. Foremost among these was Winston Churchill who returned to office as Prime Minister in 1951. His government, and subsequent Conservative administrations faced violent independence movements in Malaya, Kenya, Cyprus and Aden. The Labour government had withdrawn from Palestine and from direct involvement in most of the Middle East, although the United Kingdom retained powerful interests in Persia (Iran) and the Gulf. To many British people, however, the full knowledge of the 'end of empire' came with the débâcle of the Suez Canal in 1956.

The United Kingdom had left the militarised zone called the Canal Zone after agreement in 1954 with the new Egyptian Republic's government. The Suez Canal was owned by an Anglo-French company, mainly controlled by the British government, a major shareholder. The United States and the United Kingdom governments refused to finance the new Aswan High Dam project. Egypt obtained the money from the USSR and nationalised the Suez Canal, without compensation being agreed, in order to use the revenues to pay for the loan. The United Kingdom government, under Sir Anthony Eden, and the French government cried 'foul' and made references to dictators and appeasement. In collusion with Israel, the United Kingdom and France invaded Egypt in 1956. Egypt, which responded by blocking the canal, received United Nations' support. In the background the USSR, which was currently engaged in a bloody suppression of Hungarian democratic aspirations, made threatening noises about war. The United States, under President Eisenhower, had been kept completely in the dark about Anglo-French plans. The President and his Secretary of State, John Foster Dulles, were naturally affronted. The allied invasion was cut short when the United States government refused to help the United Kingdom financially by lending money to support the pound which was falling on the foreign exchange market. The United States also refused to support the United Kingdom's request for a loan from the International Monetary Fund which it dominated. This humiliation in late 1956 was a watershed in British political thinking. Eden resigned, ostensibly through ill health, and was succeeded in January 1957 by Harold Macmillan.

A Slow Change in the United Kingdom's Political Orientation

Eden had been a foreign affairs specialist. He had resigned as Foreign Secretary in 1938 over the policy of appeasement of Hitler, but had rejoined the Chamberlain administration on the outbreak of war as Dominions Secretary. Then he had joined the Churchill camp and returned to power on Churchill's coat-tails in 1940 as Secretary of State for War and then as Foreign Secretary. In 1951, he resumed this post and held it until succeeding to the Conservative leadership in 1955. Eden was imbued with the old doctrine of the United Kingdom's role as an imperial power and was used to hobnobbing with the great leaders of the world. His obsession with the past and his relative lack of interest in, and skill at, domestic politics was his downfall.

Macmillan, in contrast, had made his reputation as a patrician who cared about the unemployed, who understood the aspirations of ordinary folk and who had been a successful Minister of Housing and a competent Foreign Secretary and Chancellor of the Exchequer. The economic situation after the Suez débâcle was extremely serious and worsened in 1957. The fixed exchange rate of sterling was hard to maintain in the face of deepening balance of payments deficits. Large loans were necessary to support the pound. Interest rates were raised to levels unheard of except in wartime (7 per cent Bank Rate). The Suez Canal was blocked and the lack of tanker capacity severely curtailed oil supplies and raised the price of petrol. Petrol was rationed for a short time in 1957. Inflation began to rise. This period of history produces some first-rate examples of the effects of interrupted supplies upon market price, of the imposition of rationing, and of the inability of a country to maintain a fixed foreign exchange rate against determined speculation if it has insufficient reserves.

Macmillan managed to weather the economic storm but it became apparent in this period that the Six were beginning to achieve higher economic growth and were tackling some of their problems more effectively. He then began to push more rapidly towards a policy of shedding the remnants of empire, thus reducing the military and economic commitment that the colonies entailed. Macmillan started to shift the emphasis towards Europe. His famous 'wind of change' speech in Africa, in 1960, sent a shudder through the Conservative Party and there was sustained and bitter opposition to his policy of granting independence to almost all who asked. The speed of change from dependency to independent status was remarkable. Many regarded it as precipitous.

A conflict developed between those who saw Britain's future in the European context and those who saw it in an international, outward-looking role rooted in the Commonwealth and transatlantic special relationship. Some saw the European Economic Community as a narrow, self-seeking, inward-looking customs union. The issue caused splits within the parties. The anti-Common Market faction tended to attract supporters from the left and the right of British politics. They were concerned with parliamentary sovereignty, with the alleged bureaucracy of the Community and with the effects on food prices and agriculture. The impact on the poorer members of the Commonwealth and on New Zealand, which relied heavily on the United Kingdom market for its lamb sales, caused great concern. The issue of the Commonwealth Sugar Agreement loomed large, as did the future of the Commonwealth Preference system which favoured imports from, and exports to, ex-colonies. The pro-Common Market factions extolled the economies of scale available in a larger market. They welcomed what they thought would be a breath of competitive fresh air throughout British industry. They were forerunners of the Thatcherite vision of a free market, except, of course, that a more detailed study revealed the Community to be a strongly regulated market with a weak anti-monopoly policy and a powerful interventionist philosophy.

As the United Kingdom shifted its role away from colonialism, France, Belgium and Holland were also involved in disengagement from their colonial past. General de Gaulle returned to power in France in 1958, in the wake of the political chaos caused by the Algerian War. He replaced the Fourth Republic with a new constitution. Against powerful and violent opposition he settled the North African crisis. An independent Algerian state was recognised in 1962. In 1960, Belgium withdrew from the Congo. This led to a long drawn out, and bloody, civil war together with foreign intervention, before the new nations were firmly established. The Netherlands withdrew from most of their overseas possessions in the period 1949–54. France subsequently withdrew from the southern Saharan and West African states, although she has retained a powerful political and military presence in some of the countries. The rise to power of General de Gaulle, with his strongly nationalistic attitudes, was of great significance in delaying the United Kingdom's entry into the Economic Community.

De Gaulle cultivated personal aloofness and obviously believed that 'familiarity breeds contempt'. He carried this personal attitude over into his political life in attempting to restore French pride and self-esteem by an aggressively independent stance. He created a separate French nuclear strike force and withdrew from operational participation in NATO. De Gaulle wanted a restoration of the gold standard for settlement of international debts and pursued a pro-gold between nations international monetary system. He even issued silver coins, most of which quickly disappeared from circulation. In addition, he was suspicious of Anglo-American relations and treated the United Kingdom's avowed aspiration to be 'European' with scepticism. There was much reference to 'perfidious Albion'.

In October 1961, the United Kingdom made its first formal

application to join the EEC. Negotiations took place which ended in January 1963 when de Gaulle exercised his personal veto, on behalf of France, against Britain's application for membership. His remarks about the United Kingdom not being truly European were a reflection of his intense anger at the Nassau Agreement of December 1962 between Macmillan and President Kennedy. This agreement was for the USA to supply missiles for British nuclear submarines, that is the Polaris system. Ironically, Macmillan had been forced into the Nassau Agreement by the failure of a proposed independent British nuclear weapons delivery system. The French veto was a severe blow to Macmillan, and it also blocked the applications of Denmark, Norway and Ireland.

Macmillan resigned because of ill-health in October 1963 and was succeeded by his Foreign Secretary, the Earl of Home, who renounced his peerage in order to become an MP. Home was a foreign affairs expert and was, self-confessedly, not an economist. His government was narrowly defeated by Labour, under Harold Wilson, in October 1964. Wilson called another election in March 1966 and received a greatly enlarged majority. The whole course of his government was dominated by balance of payments problems and the necessity of maintaining the pound at its fixed level. Economic growth was slow and attempts at national planning quickly foundered. Envious eyes were cast on the successful French system of indicative planning and at the higher rates of growth and lower inflation rates of the EEC. Thus despite strong ideological objections from the left wing of the Labour Party, Wilson applied for the United Kingdom to join the Community in 1967. This second application of the United Kingdom, together with those of Denmark, Norway and Ireland, was again rejected by de Gaulle in 1967. The way was blocked until de Gaulle resigned his office in April 1969 after badly misjudging the mood of the French people over a referendum to modify the constitution.

EFTA

There was a nine-month gap between the signing of the Treaties of Rome in March 1957 and their coming into force on 1 January 1958. The United Kingdom used this period to try to establish a different type of organisation, a European Free Trade Association among the seventeen members of the OEEC. Such a market would be free from tariffs and trade barriers between members but would allow each country to set its own trade conditions with non-members. This would combine the benefits of a partial customs union with the advantage of no loss of sovereignty to the member. It was a 'partial' customs union because it did not have a common external tariff. The system appealed to countries which favoured political neutrality and to the United Kingdom which had obligations to its Commonwealth friends. It did not, however, satisfy the basic desire of the six signatories of the Rome treaties because they wanted deeper political involvement and commitment, with a view to obviating any future European war. France was strongly opposed to the British initiative and ended discussions in November 1958. When EFTA was formed by the Stockholm Convention of November 1959 its membership was the United Kingdom, Austria, Denmark, Norway, Portugal, Sweden and Switzerland. Iceland became a full member in March 1970. Finland became an associate member in July 1961. EFTA became operational in May 1960. Over the years its membership has fluctuated as countries joined and/or left to join the EEC instead. The 1988 membership was Austria, Finland, Iceland, Norway, Sweden and Switzerland. There are close working agreements between the Community and EFTA and these are being redrawn as the completion of the single European market, aimed at 1992, draws closer.

Britain quickly realised that EFTA would not satisfy its economic and political needs in a changing world. Its markets were not large enough for sufficient economies of scale to be derived, compared with the EEC markets. More importantly, it did not provide sufficient opportunity for the United Kingdom to exercise its political weight. The United Kingdom was in danger of becoming a politically isolated off-shore island near the continent of Europe. An alternative future was as an undeclared state of the American Union, dependent on the USA economically and politically. The so-called 'special relationship' between the United Kingdom and the United States had never been one of equals but no one wanted it to degenerate into an overtly master–vassal relationship.

EFTA is very different in operation from the European Community. It is run by weekly meetings of officials and meetings of ministers two or three times a year. There are no powers devolved by each country on a central organisation so there is nothing supranational about it. It has been successful in abolishing almost all import duties on industrial goods between members and has generally harmonised its external tariffs with those of the EEC. It was expected that the departure of the United Kingdom on joining the EEC would see the end of EFTA but that has not happened.

The United Kingdom's Successful Application

Soon after the fall of de Gaulle in April 1969, his successor, President Pompidou, made it clear that his government would not object in principle to the entry of Britain and the other applicants provided that enlargement would strengthen rather than weaken the Community. In December 1969, a summit was held at The Hague. This agreed to major alterations in the way that the Community was to be financed and developed; it also agreed to prepare for negotiations on its enlargement. In May 1970, the Labour government announced that it would restart negotiations as soon as possible. There was a change of government in June 1970 and the Conservatives under Mr Heath began negotiations at the end of June. The continuity of policy irrespective of governing party is shown clearly by the fact that the negotiations were on the lines prepared by the Labour government. Within a year the negotiations were complete except on the issue of fisheries.

There was no United Kingdom referendum on entry to the EEC. In the 1960s and early 1970s the only referendums held were on whether Welsh public houses should open on the Sabbath! Although there was eventually a referendum in June 1975 called by the Labour government on whether the United Kingdom should *remain* in the Community, the original entry was by decision of the House of Commons. In May 1967, the Labour government had announced its decision to apply for membership. There was a three-day debate which ended in a vote in favour of the application of 488 to 62. This majority of 426 is one of the largest ever majorities of the House of Commons in peacetime. This fact has tended to be obscured over the years as more and more politicians have found it expedient to side with the critics of the development of the Community. Those who objected at the time did so on grounds of fear for national or parliamentary sovereignty, on fears for the Commonwealth relationship, or on sectional interest grounds related to agriculture or fishing. They were drawn from both extremes of the political spectrum.

When it was decided to reapply for membership in 1970 a new White Paper, 'Britain and the European Communities: An Economic Assessment' (Cmnd 4289), was published in February 1970. This updated the figures of likely costs and benefits of membership, concluding that the economic balance was a fine one and that in the short term there would be some economic disadvantages. The range of figures given for possible balance of payments changes, agricultural expenditure changes and alterations in capital movements was very wide. The statisticians had to make many assumptions about such variables as growth rates, patterns of trade and agricultural prices. In general, the conclusion was that it was the long-term economic advantages and, even more, the political advantages, which would prove decisive. In the background was the knowledge that it was impossible to calculate the full economic consequences of *not* entering the European Community: these consequences were in terms of being both excluded from and being in competition with an increasingly integrated European economy, on our doorsteps, and several times the size and probably faster growing than our own. It was also impossible to quantify the so-called 'dynamic' effects resulting from membership of a much larger and faster growing market. The sorts of figures which had a powerful persuasive effect were comparative growth figures like those in Tables 3.1 and 3.2.

The figures were presented in a more readily understood form in a nationally distributed booklet, 'Britain and Europe', which explained the government's White Paper 'The United Kingdom and the European Communities' (Cmnd 4715) as in Table 3.2.

The Entry Terms

The terms negotiated for entry on almost all major points were published in a White Paper in July 1971. In October 1971, the House of Commons voted by 356 to 244 in favour of joining the EEC on these terms. In January 1972, the Treaty of Accession was signed and the resulting European Communities Act received the royal assent in October 1972, after a fairly stormy passage through Parliament.

The agreement fixed a transitional period of five years from the

TABLE 3.1
Growth of GNP per head at 1963 Market Prices, 1958–67

	Average annual % increase			
EEC countries			*EFTA countries*	
West Germany	3.7	United Kingdom	2.5
France	3.9	Sweden	3.8
Italy	4.8	Norway	4.0
Belgium	3.8	Denmark	4.2
Luxembourg	n.a.	Austria	3.7
Netherlands	3.7	Switzerland	3.1
		Portugal	5.2
Average all EEC countries	4.0*	Average all EFTA countries	3.0*

* At 1963 exchange rates.
SOURCE 'Britain and the European Communities: An Economic Assessment', Cmnd 4289 (London: HMSO, 1970).

TABLE 3.2
Increase **in Average Income per Employed Person in Real Terms, 1958–69**

Italy	> > > > > > > > > > > > > > > > > > 92%
France	> > > > > > > > > > > > > > > 77%
Netherlands	> > > > > > > > > > > > > > 74%
West Germany	> > > > > > > > > > > > > 72%
Belgium	> > > > > > > > > > > 52%
Britain	> > > > > > > > > 39%
Average EEC	> > > > > > > > > > > > > 76%

start of Britain's membership on 1 January 1973 to 31 December 1977. In that period all tariffs between Britain and the Six were to be abolished in five equal stages, so that within three years of entry there would be virtually free access to the European market for British exporters.

Agriculture required very detailed terms involving a gradual increase in market prices so that direct subsidy payment to farmers (in the form of deficiency payments) could be phased out. The government kept the power to help groups such as hill farmers and to retain the marketing boards. It was anticipated that agricultural output would increase by about 8 per cent over the transitional five years as home production was substituted for imports. A special agreement was made so that New Zealand could continue to have access to the British market for at least 75 per cent of its current exports of butter and cheese to Europe until the end of the transitional period. Similarly, the United Kingdom retained its obligations under the Commonwealth Sugar Agreement to buy agreed quantities of sugar from existing sources until 1974 and to protect the relationship thereafter. This was to quell well-substantiated fears that Caribbean cane-producing countries would suffer if the United Kingdom were forced to buy European beet sugar.

The question of budget contributions was resolved by fixing the British part of the total budget as a gradually rising percentage, from 8.64 per cent in 1973 to 18.92 per cent in 1977.

There were additional agreements on the free movement of labour, regional development, the Coal and Steel Community, and Euratom. In most cases, the United Kingdom accepted existing practices without reservation, although Northern Ireland was excluded from free movement of labour for five years. Commonwealth countries in Africa, the Indian Ocean, the Pacific and the Caribbean were offered 'association' with the EEC in order to protect access for their exports to the Community. Australia and Canada were not thought to require any special arrangements.

Renegotiation and the Referendum

A significant number of important persons and groups within the Labour Party were against the United Kingdom's membership of the EEC. This opposition went so far as to prevent any Labour Party representatives going to the European Parliament (until July 1975). As a result of this pressure the party manifesto at the February 1974 general election promised that the electorate should have the opportunity of deciding on whether Britain should stay as a member or not. The new Labour government under Wilson, therefore, began talks in April 1974 for renegotiation of the terms of membership. These were concluded in March 1975 and Parliament endorsed the terms of the agreement on a free vote by 396 votes to 170 in early April.

This was a rather confusing period politically and indicates the extent to which the European Community concept split the parties. Mrs Thatcher became Leader of the Opposition in February 1975 after the fall of Mr Heath who was the great champion of membership and who, according to his critics, was willing to accept any terms, however harsh, for entry. The Prime Minister, Mr Wilson, was having trouble within his party and had to accept the idea of giving his Cabinet colleagues a 'licence to differ' instead of insisting on the traditional doctrine of collective responsibility. As a result, on the free vote in the House of Commons, the 396 votes in favour of remaining in the EEC consisted of 249 Conservatives, 135 Labour and 12 Liberals. The 170 votes against were 144 Labour, 7 Conservative, 11 Scottish Nationalist, 6 Ulster Unionist and 2 Plaid Cymru. No fewer than seven Labour Cabinet ministers voted against, together with thirty other ministers.

The Labour Party responded to this Commons vote by calling a special Labour Party Conference at the end of April. This approved a recommendation from the National Executive Committee that Britain should leave the EEC. The party was not happy with the renegotiated terms: the voting was 3 724 000 to 1 986 000. A few days earlier, the TUC had adopted a document opposing the United Kingdom's continued membership, although individual unions were left free to express different opinions.

The solution for the government was to lie in the promised referendum. This took place on 5 June 1975. Voters had to vote 'yes' or 'no' to the question 'Do you think that the United Kingdom should stay in the European Community (the Common Market)?' The overall result was a 67.2 per cent vote of 'yes' but there were significant regional differences as can be seen in Table 3.3.

The organisation representing each side of the argument was given £125 000 by the government to conduct their campaign and every household received three pamphlets, one from each side and one from the government putting its side of the case. 'The National Referendum Campaign' which organised the groups that were against continued membership spent £131 000. The pro-market group 'Britain in Europe' spent £1 482 000 and conducted a much slicker campaign with more effective advertising.

TABLE 3.3
The Referendum of June 1975

	% *Turnout*	% *'Yes'*
England	64.6	68.7
Wales	66.7	64.8
Scotland	61.7	58.4
Northern Ireland	47.4	52.1
United Kingdom	64.5	67.2

Only the Shetland Isles (56.3% 'No') and the Western Isles (70.5% 'No') voted against.

The resounding and unequivocal 'yes' vote cleared the air and national energies could now be devoted to making Britain's membership work to the nation's greatest benefit. Despite this, membership of the Community was often made a scapegoat for problems which were already deeply ingrained in Britain's industrial and social structures. The early years of transitional membership coincided with rapidly rising unemployment, swift decline of manufacturing industry, poor industrial relations, international inflation and recession, and uncertainty in politics. Inevitably, the Common Market was thought by some to exacerbate these problems. The Labour Party, for some years, promised withdrawal from the Community if it were re-elected to government. In 1983, however, it modified this stance and made withdrawal 'an option' rather than a certainty if it should be returned to power. The Conservative Party, for its part, concentrated upon altering the budgetary imbalance and on pursuing an aggressively self-interested national policy. General de Gaulle might very well have admired Mrs Thatcher's approach although there often seems to be a major discrepancy between what was agreed between the members and what the British public was told had been achieved. In December 1979, Mrs Thatcher, at the Dublin summit meeting, asked for 'Britain's money back'. There was a short-term palliative agreement in 1980 but it was not until the Fontainebleau agreement in June 1984 that there was a full settlement of the United Kingdom's grievance (see Chapter 9). The figures in Table 3.4 support the validity of the sense of injustice.

TABLE 3.4
United Kingdom's Contributions and Receipts from the Community Budget (£ millions)

	Gross contributions	Receipts	Net contributions
1973	181	79	102
1974	181	150	31
1975	342	398	− 56
1976	463	296	167
1977	737	368	368
1978	1348	544	804
1979	1606	659	947
1980	1767	1061	710
1981	2174	1777	997
1982	2863	2257	606
1983*	3120	2473	647

* Estimates.
SOURCE 'The Government Expenditure Plans, 1977–78 to 1982–83', Cmnd 7439 (London: HMSO, 1984), quoted in Butler, D. E., *British Political Facts, 1980–85*, 6th edn (London: Macmillan, 1986).

Governing the One Europe 4

This chapter will be better understood if the details of the main channels of decision-making in the Community, as outlined in Chapter 1 under the heading 'Decision-making in the Community', are consulted. Figure 4.1 summarises these relationships.

Such Figures as 4.1 give only a broad impression of where decisions are actually made. Ministers are advised by their civil servants. As a result, departmental policy refined over time is frequently more powerful than an individual minister who may have only a short stay in office. The officials of the Commission are also career civil servants who have a profound long-term effect on Commission policy. The Commissioners usually serve for four years and some serve more than one term. They may, however, switch portfolios because these are reshuffled every four years. A very important role in decision-making is played by a committee called COREPER, the Committee of Permanent Representatives, which comprises the Ambassadors to the Community and their advisors and is the vital link between member governments and the Community. What may be said definitively is that no decision can be finally reached except by the Council of Ministers. How they reach that decision and whether they are sometimes a 'rubber stamp' depends on their personalities, the detail of the proposals and political factors.

50

FIGURE 4.1
How a Decision Is Taken in the European Community

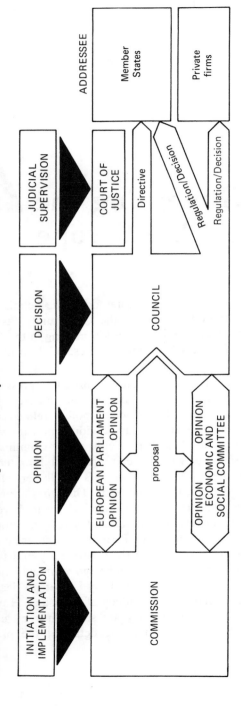

SOURCE   Eurostat, *Europe in Figures* (Luxembourg: Office for the Official Publications of the European Communities, 1988).

Unanimous or Majority Decisions?

The Treaty of Rome required decisions to be made unanimously in the Council of Ministers. This gave each nation an effective veto. The system which was intended to protect a nation's vital self-interest (as seen by itself) became less sensible as the Community was enlarged. The Single European Act which was signed in 1986 and came into force in July 1987 therefore included the provision for a qualified majority decision. This applies to measures which have as their object the establishment and functioning of the internal market and will prevent delays imposed by a single reluctant member. The qualified majority system will not apply to every area of Community decision-making; the Council must remain unanimous when dealing with revenue, taxation and social policy. Majority voting does apply to transport, the environment and other matters related to the establishment of the internal market. The details of the qualified majority system in the Council of Ministers are shown in Table 4.1. These weighted voting powers enable a single important state to be outvoted but enable two large states together to prevent policies being implemented against their wills. The system prevents total

TABLE 4.1
Votes

West Germany	10
France	10
Italy	10
UK	10
Spain	8
Belgium	5
Greece	5
Netherlands	5
Portugal	5
Denmark	3
Ireland	3
Luxembourg	2
TOTAL	76
Qualified majority	54

obstructionism by one state but encourages dealing between nations to modify or promote policies.

What Is the Problem of National Sovereignty?

Each nation, because it is an internationally recognised separate entity, has institutions which constitutionally have the power to make decisions on its behalf. This power of decision-making may be called sovereignty. Most nations have written constitutions and it is clearly laid out in them which bodies make laws and which court can vet those laws constitutionally. All nations at some time have chosen to subjugate this power of decision-making to some form of international agreement such as the Universal Declaration of Human Rights, or the European Convention on Human Rights, or the Geneva Convention on behaviour in war. Theoretically they retain the right to withdraw their agreement thus retaining their national sovereignty. In practice, however, such a withdrawal would be politically unthinkable in normal circumstances. This does not, of course, prevent some regimes ignoring or flagrantly flouting human rights. Yet they all, eventually, are subject to the international law to which they have subscribed.

In some forms of agreements some states have gone much further in surrendering the power of decision-making to other bodies. The best examples lie with the various federal governments that exist, as in the United States of America, the Federal Republic of West Germany or the Union of Soviet Socialist Republics. In the American federal system the individual states voluntarily surrendered certain decision-making powers to the federal government consisting of President and Congress. The more important of these powers were the making of foreign policy, national defence, the currency and the regulation of interstate commerce. Note that the states gave the right. It is not a system where the federal government has all power and deigns to delegate some to the states. Some people persist in putting forward the view that the future for the European Community lies with a federal system. There seems to be relatively little support for this and many would say that there is no real need because the Community has been developed in a unique way to render federation unnecessary.

Most of the members of the Community have suffered from

foreign occupation, whether from Napoleon or from Prussia and Hitler's Germany. Most have experienced the need for coalition governments and compromise in decision-making. Some are small states which have always existed under the shadow of their larger, more powerful neighbours. Too much dwelling on theoretical ideals of sovereignty is, to them, a waste of time. They all took the pragmatic line which led to the signing of the European Coal and Steel Community (ECSC) Treaty and the Treaties of Rome. In these they set up institutions which made decisions affecting wide areas of their national lives, especially in the economic sphere. They set up the Court of Justice to judge the constitutionality of decisions made by member states, the European Commission, Parliament and Council of Ministers. This 'surrender of sovereignty' was made with open eyes and in frank recognition that the sacrifice of some degree of independence was essential if the great ideal of a Europe without strife and poverty was to be achieved. Opinion in the United Kingdom was not influenced by the same historical factors and was less pragmatic. 'Sovereignty' is still an important issue in some areas of British political debate.

The United Kingdom has no written constitution although certain laws and documents are part of its constitution. There is a great contrast in the United Kingdom between the 'formal' parts of the constitution, Queen and Privy Council for example, and the 'effective' parts, namely the Prime Minister and Cabinet. The role of the United Kingdom Parliament is very debatable nowadays. It has become increasingly 'formal' as its willingness to check the executive has waned and as the ability of the government to control through the whip system has increased. Yet, in the final analysis, Parliament, or the 'Crown in Parliament' to be pedantic, is sovereign. A Parliament can, in theory, undo any act of any of its predecessors. No Parliament can bind its successors. In practical politics, however, things are different. The United Kingdom government and Parliament are irrevocably committed to those international conventions which are compatible with what all Britons are alleged to hold dear – freedoms of expression, property, religion, etc. They accept international law and generally follow United Nations edicts. The room for genuine independence or sovereignty had been increasingly constrained over the centuries. All this did not prevent a major outcry about 'loss of sovereignty' if the United Kingdom signed the Treaty of Rome and joined the European Community. This outcry was repeated, in minor vein, when the Single European Act was passed in 1986. It seems to be very difficult for some groups of British politicians and journalists to accept the idea that the United Kingdom can, and has, voluntarily given powers of decision to European institutions in which we may have only one-twelfth of a say. The United Kingdom Parliament is then relegated to a rubber-stamping function. It has failed to create sufficiently good vetting and criticising committees to monitor European legislation so that it might have a more positive role. The House of Commons is considering introducing a special Question Time on a regular basis to deal with Community matters.

The government has, for the sake of an easy life in getting its measures through Parliament, connived at this emasculation of the British legislature. Yet, in the hypocritical way of governments, leading United Kingdom politicians have not hesitated to wave the stick of 'threats to British or parliamentary sovereignty' when their policies are frustrated on the European mainland. There has been a tendency to resort to sovereignty as an excuse for stalling or obstructionism when the other eleven members of the Community have agreed on a policy. Patriotism is said to be 'the last refuge of a scoundrel'. It could also be said that sovereignty is the penultimate refuge.

It is possible to defend the government's approach in pushing the Single European Act through Parliament yet, later, arguing on the grounds of sovereignty and national interest against the logical outcomes of the Act. The defence is on the grounds of expediency. The government was fully aware of the extent to which it was surrendering sovereignty to the Council of Ministers, the Commission and the European Parliament but it knew that public opinion could easily be whipped up against such a surrender. It therefore played this aspect down and concentrated on the positive economic benefits of harmonisation and the removal of barriers. Once the necessary legislation was passed, it has found it expedient to calm public fears about specific measures by quoting the national interest and sovereignty in its arguments with its European partners. It has done this over sensitive proposals about border controls, VAT, harmonisation, and joining the Exchange Rate Mechanism of the EMS. Increasingly, however, in a multitude of day-to-day decisions the issue of sovereignty is becoming irrelevant. The legislation has been agreed to, the power delegated and the individual nation's veto is largely a thing of the past.

Will Sovereignty Be an Issue in the Future?

The issue of sovereignty will never go away completely because groups of people and nations will always come to feel at some time that they could do better if they made all their decisions for themselves. There is, for example, a Basque separatist movement, a Walloon independence movement and similar aspirations in Cornwall, Wales, Scotland and the Italian Alps. It is easy to dismiss these trends as the stirrings of adolescent independence. They represent attitudes which arise in any arrangement that has dominant partners. It will be inevitable, therefore, that as the effects of the creation of a genuine single European market become understood that there will be two major strands of opinion developing.

One will say 'haven't things worked out well, and look what can be achieved by close cooperation and common objectives – let's try to achieve even closer political harmony in a federal structure'. They will want a common currency, a single central bank, a Community police force and perhaps a Community defence and foreign policy.

The second strand of opinion will say 'look at the negative effects, the growth of regional disparities, look how badly we have done and see how the big nations dominate decision-making at our expense. Let's go our own way.' The Treaty of Rome is rather exceptional in that it does not provide any means by which a signatory can leave the Community. It appears to be an irrevocable decision. Despite this Greenland chose, after a referendum, to separate itself from Denmark in this context and to negotiate a separate associate status. The Community is not likely to wish to restrain a member who wants to leave.

Such polarisation of opinion is, of course, speculative and possibly exaggerated and a great deal will depend on how the Community institutions perform over the next few years, particularly the Parliament.

Will the European Parliament Be Adequate in the Future?

The European Parliament has become more effective since its powers were extended slightly under the Single European Act of 1986 and, more particularly, since its indirect election system was replaced by direct universal suffrage in 1979. Many British MEPs

(Members of the European Parliament) take the rather parochial view that it was the advent of the British with their long parliamentary tradition that changed the nature of the European Parliament. The Parliament has 518 members elected by proportional representation, except in Great Britain where the election is still by the traditional first past the post method. Northern Ireland uses the Single Transferable Vote system of proportional representation to elect its MEPs. Many MEPs, except from the United Kingdom, do not have a specific constituency to which they are directly accountable. This reduces their work burden and their direct contact with the people. The Parliament divides into groups by political tendency rather than by nationality. MEPs are increasingly subjected to the approaches of pressure groups of different types despite the fact that their powers are very restricted.

The European Parliament's powers are very much less than those of national Parliaments. Its main job is to oversee and approve the work of the Commission. It can vote the Commission out of office with a two-thirds majority but the relationship between Parliament and Commission is such as to make this event extremely unlikely. Parliament has relatively little control over the budget although it must give its approval and can propose certain increases. It cannot itself create new sources of revenue. Since 1979 the Parliament has become more effective in criticising the Commission and Council of Ministers through its questions and committee system. It has been helped in the area of the budget by the twelve-member Court of Auditors which supervises the implementation of the budget.

The above is necessarily a brief analysis of the European Parliament's power. MEPs tend to give a rosier picture of their effectiveness and that of the Parliament. Some critics would be much more damning and allege that the Parliament is a self-important talking shop with the minimum of influence over decision-making. Its quaint movements between Strasbourg, Brussels and Luxembourg do not help its efficiency, although this may eventually be ended and the Parliament may settle in Brussels.

It is likely that the European Parliament will gradually try to increase its role and influence. There is plenty of evidence since 1986 that this is the trend. If the United Kingdom introduces proportional representation in European elections, as it should eventually do, then there may be an injection of more 'democratic' blood into the Parliament. As the single market extends and intensifies, the electorate of Europe and pressure groups will increasingly look to the European Parliament rather than to national Parliaments. Each national bureaucracy will also increasingly work through European channels. Over time the European Parliament will be seen to be more important and will almost certainly want more powers. It may prove to be the best defence of democracy for the British people whose own Parliament has become decayed and ineffectual.

Is the Community Bureaucratic?

The word 'bureaucratic' is often used as a term of abuse by critics of an institution or system. It is frequently used with reference to the Community. Articles which dwell on the 'bureaucratic' nature of the Community usually include a picture of the Berlaymont Building in Brussels which houses the headquarters of the Commission. This is a cross-shaped office block of about twelve storeys with a circular helicopter pad on top at the intersection of the cross. Near it is the smaller Charlemagne Building which is used for the Council of Ministers. Articles on a similar theme about the United States frequently include a photograph of the Pentagon.

The word 'bureaucratic' has two main meanings when used critically. The first is that the number of employees engaged in administrative tasks is excessive in relation to the size of the whole organisation or to the task in hand. (A classic case is the British Navy which now has more Admirals than large surface ships.) The implication is that many will be engaged in pointless and repetitive clerical tasks which hold up the implementation of policy. The Community definitely does not suffer from this kind of bureaucracy. It employs only about 20 000 employees. The administrative cost of the Community is only about 4.6 per cent of the budget of which the Commission takes up 2.98 per cent, the Council 0.41 per cent and Parliament 0.81 per cent. These figures may, of course, be regarded as simply the tip of the iceberg. The individual member states employ many others on Community related work and the implementation of its policies. They are, however, counted as national civil servants and not as Community employees.

The other meaning given to the word 'bureaucratic' is more nebulous and implies a ponderous, labyrinthine decision-making process with a complex hierarchy that causes decision-making to be delayed. It is obvious that the Community, comprising twelve nations, might lend itself to this type of bureaucracy because proposals and decisions have to be constantly referred back and forth between the individual states and the Community institutions. There is no real evidence, though, that the Community is more bureaucratic than it need be. It can be argued that it is highly efficient and effective in its decision-making processes, even allowing for the inevitable time delay required for compromises. Its achievements in meeting deadlines in the drafting and passing of directives for the coming of the single European market by 1992 have been impressive, achieving most of the 300 measures well on schedule. There are currently (in early 1989) a few major areas of dispute such as merger policy, banking regulation and border controls that may delay matters, but past experience indicates that these problems will be resolved in time. In this sense of the word 'bureaucratic', as discussed in this paragraph, it may be said that Europe is nowhere near as bureaucratic as the United States or the Soviet Union.

In the context of the 'bureaucratic' criticism, some people hope that the creation of the single European market will remove a great deal of administrative work. This has already happened with the use of a single document for commercial vehicles crossing internal frontiers of the Community. The abolition in many sectors of such controls as those on capital movements and the harmonisation of regulations should both help reduce bureaucracy. There is a fear, though, that a new structure of rules, regulations and controls will actually establish a tighter and, eventually, more extensive bureaucracy. Mrs Thatcher has expressed this fear especially in the context of social policy and tax harmonisation. Her view of an extension of free market forces is increasingly at variance with the Common European and Community view of a benevolent guiding hand or direct interventionist role for the state.

A Budget Problem – Where to Get the Money

Community budget problems have changed in nature over the years. The most persistent, until 1988, was that revenues never matched the levels of expenditure required to meet all the desirable objectives. The Community budget is fundamentally different from national budgets in that it is not an instrument of economic policy using deficits or surpluses to achieve economic objectives. As expenditure under the agricultural programmes got out of control, especially on the price guarantee side, there were less resources available for regional, social and technological programmes. The budget became the cause of annual conflicts between the Commission and the European Parliament and between nations at the Council of Ministers. All sorts of expedients and varieties of creative accountancy were adopted as temporary palliatives. When, eventually, the issue of controlling agricultural payments was successfully met in 1987–8, there was more scope for sensible budgetary policies.

At the same time, there was a welcome increase in revenues for the Community from January 1986. This resulted from the decision in 1984 to increase the VAT revenues payable to the Community by each member to the equivalent of a 1.4 per cent rate of a uniform basis of assessment. This decision, implemented in January 1986, has provided much needed extra revenue and there may be pressure in the future to increase this percentage further. The percentage was originally 1 per cent from 1970 to 1983. Since VAT receipts constitute about 60 per cent of the Community's income, they yield the greatest return if the rate of contribution is increased.

The Community's revenues also began to take a healthier turn after the Brussels agreement in February 1988. The national leaders agreed to have additional national contributions to the revenues based on relative national wealth (GNP). They allowed the Community to collect up to 1.2 per cent of GNP. This very welcome increase in potential revenue, together with the rise in VAT contributions, permitted a rise of up to 30 per cent in the revenues over time, compared with the 1987 budget.

In its early days, between 1957 and 1970, the Community's revenue was based on contributions from the six members paid in accordance with an agreed scale based on shares of Gross National Product and other criteria. As was always intended by the Treaty of Rome, the Community shifted its revenue base once the Common Customs Tariff (CCT) was introduced in mid 1968. After the 1970 Hague summit the Community developed a system of revenue from 'its own resources' – that is it was guaranteed money from specific sources. At this time the United Kingdom, Ireland and Denmark were in the process of joining so the changes took place over some years. These sources were: customs duties, agricultural levies, sugar levies and a percentage of the VAT receipts.

The change-over to 'own-resources' financing was slow in several respects; it was only speedy in relation to sugar levies. These charges on the production and storage of sugar were transferred to the Community in 1971. They were extended to isoglucose in 1977. The money is used to finance support in the markets for sugar. In the case of customs revenue the complete transfer of all revenues to the Community was not achieved until 1975. Even then customs duties on coal and steel were not handed over to the Community.

Revenue from customs duties has been of decreasing relative importance because of the series of international GATT talks which have reduced tariffs – i.e. the Kennedy round (1962–7), the Tokyo round (1980–7) and the Uruguay round (1988). Various other agreements have also cut customs revenues – the Lome agreement, for example, and bilateral agreements with Mediterranean countries. The general rise in imports and their prices has not compensated for this general decline in tariff levels. If, as the single market develops, the Community successfully replaces imports with home produced products, then it can expect a further reduction in its revenues from tariffs. The member states keep 10 per cent of the revenue from customs duties and agricultural levies in order to meet administration and collection costs.

The transfer of agricultural levies also took place over the years 1971–5. These levies are placed upon imported agricultural products to bring their prices up to the level of the Community products' prices. The revenue from them depends on price movements and exchange rates. The United Kingdom, being a relatively large importer of food products, contributes disproportionately to agricultural levies. They are not a very good source of revenue because they tend to fluctuate unpredictably. The revenue from them goes to help support or intervention buying within the Community but it is nowhere near sufficient for this purpose. Table 4.2 illustrates the problem as it was in 1985.

It was decided in 1970 to make VAT the main source of the Community's own revenue, but it was not until the budget of 1980 that every member paid its full VAT payments. Proceedings before the Court of Justice were required to make Ireland, Italy, Luxembourg and Germany comply in 1979 with the sixth VAT Directive of May 1977. The members agreed to give the Community up to 1 per cent of a uniform basis of assessment of value added tax. This limit was raised to 1.4 per cent in January 1986 after the Fontainebleau

TABLE 4.2
The Community Budget, 1985 (percentage)

Receipts		Expenditure	
VAT	55.5	Agriculture and fisheries	72.9
Customs duties	29.6	Regional policy	5.9
Non-repayable advances	5.9	Social policy	5.7
Agricultural levies	4.0	Development	
Sugar and isoglucose		cooperation	3.9
levies	3.8	Research, energy,	
Miscellaneous	1.2	transport	2.6
		Administrative costs	4.6
		Miscellaneous	4.4

Total payment appropriations + 28 000 million ECU

summit resolved the United Kingdom's contribution problem. There is pressure to raise the figure further but the United Kingdom and Germany are reluctant because they think that the limit imposes more budgetary discipline on the Community, particularly on the agricultural budget.

VAT was chosen as a source of revenue because the sixth VAT Directive of May 1977 harmonised the turnover (or VAT) systems. The tax is paid by all Community citizens and its revenue closely reflects the economic capacity of each member state. This may be regarded as an equitable system and is, to a degree, progressive because high revenue from VAT reflects high levels of consumption which, in turn, reflects high disposable incomes. The amount paid is based on a uniform basis of assessment defined as 'the sum of all taxable supplies of goods and services to the final consumer in the Community'. This means that it does not depend on the VAT rates which continue to differ quite widely among member states. As part of the progress towards the creation of the single European market in 1992 it was intended to try to harmonise VAT rates. This will probably not happen fully for a long time after 1992. Some compromise on bands of rates is likely in the short term. The United

Kingdom government is opposed to full harmonisation of rates of VAT because it would have to impose the tax on goods at present exempt, notably food and children's clothing. It has, however, quietly extended VAT in 1988 and 1989 to some areas hitherto excluded, such as opticians' services and parts of the construction industry. The French too are opposed to full harmonisation because they would have to lower many of their rates and find alternative sources of revenue.

The details of the 1989 budget and a comparative study of the changes in the budget between 1973 and 1989 are given in Tables 4.3, 4.4 and Figure 4.2. The national contributions to the Community's revenues are given in Table 4.5.

How Are the Budget and Exchange Rate Fluctuations Reconciled?

The Community needed to devise a system for payments between members and the Community to take account of changes in foreign exchange rates. Before 1977 budgets were drawn up and implemented in terms of 'units of account' (u.a.). Each u.a. was equivalent to a fine ounce of gold – this was the content of the US dollar between 1934 and 1972. In other words, the exchange rate in relation to the US dollar was the basis of calculation. Between 1978 and 1980 the European Unit of Account (EUA) was used instead and was based on a 'basket' of currencies. Since 1980 the budget has been drawn up and executed in terms of the ECU (European Currency Unit). This is described and explained fully in Chapter 7. The ECU is based upon a 'basket' of currencies in which individual currencies are weighted according to objective measures such as a country's share of the Community's Gross Domestic Product, and share of Community trade. This weighting is reviewed every five years. From 1979–80 the ECU was used for all legal and financial purposes and in the budget from January 1981.

The value of the ECU is worked out on a daily basis for each country's currency in relation to the currency's standing on the exchange markets. The Community budget is drawn up each year using the ECU rates for 1 February of the previous year. For example, the 1989 budget was drawn up on the ECU rate prevailing on 1 February 1988.

TABLE 4.3
General Community Budget: Revenue Forecast for 1989

	Million ECU	%
Customs duties	9 954	22.2
Agricultural levies	2 462	5.4
VAT	26 219	58.5
GNP resource	3 907	8.7
Miscellaneous	274	0.6
Balance from previous financial year	2 025	4.5
	44 841 (or 1.03% of Community GNP)	

SOURCE   European File, 'The European Community Budget' (Luxembourg: Office for Official Publications of the European Communities, 1989).

TABLE 4.4
European Community Expenditure by Sector (per cent)

	1981	*1986*	*1988*
Agriculture and fisheries	65.1	67.2	71.8
Regional policy	12.6	7.6	7.3
Social policy	4.7	7.1	6.4
Cooperation with developing countries	4.8	2.5	1.8
Research, energy, industry, transport	2.1	2.5	2.4
Reimbursement to member states	5.4	8.7	6.1
Administration	5.3	4.4	4.0

SOURCE   Eurostat, *Basic Statistics of the Community*, 25th edn (Luxembourg: Office for the Official Publications of the European Communities, 1988).

FIGURE 4.2

1. Development of the General Community budget, 1973–89

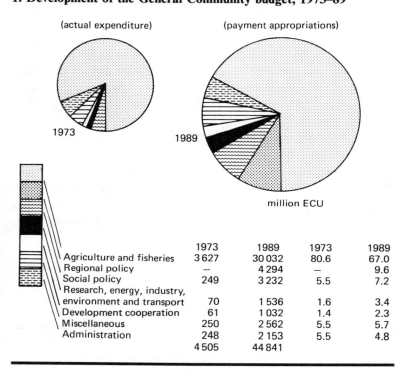

(actual expenditure)   (payment appropriations)

1973   1989

million ECU

	1973	1989	1973	1989
Agriculture and fisheries	3 627	30 032	80.6	67.0
Regional policy	–	4 294	–	9.6
Social policy	249	3 232	5.5	7.2
Research, energy, industry, environment and transport	70	1 536	1.6	3.4
Development cooperation	61	1 032	1.4	2.3
Miscellaneous	250	2 562	5.5	5.7
Administration	248	2 153	5.5	4.8
	4 505	44 841		

The use of the ECU was important in enabling monetary compensatory amounts (MCAs) to be calculated and adjusted. These were payments introduced in 1971 for agricultural products as they crossed frontiers to compensate for changes in exchange rates or the adjustment in central rates in the days before 1979 when the European Monetary System was introduced. The system was extremely complicated and involved the calculation of a 'green' rate for each currency – hence talk of the 'green pound', or the 'green mark'. The whole system created great problems at the annual discussion of the level of agricultural support prices. There were positive and negative MCAs depending on the movement of currencies. MCAs were a large burden on the Community's budget. The

2. Financial Forecasts, 1988–92 (commitment appropriations, million ECU)

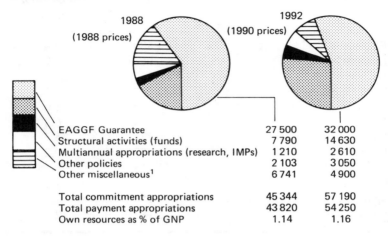

	1988	1992
EAGGF Guarantee	27 500	32 000
Structural activities (funds)	7 790	14 630
Multiannual appropriations (research, IMPs)	1 210	2 610
Other policies	2 103	3 050
Other miscellaneous[1]	6 741	4 900
Total commitment appropriations	45 344	57 190
Total payment appropriations	43 820	54 250
Own resources as % of GNP	1.14	1.16

[1] Reimbursements to Member States, monetary reserve, administrative costs, etc.

SOURCE European File 'The European Community Budget' (Luxembourg: Office for Official Publications of the European Communities, 1989).

balance between positive and negative MCAs constituted about 10 per cent of the expenditure on price guarantees.

In 1984–5, a new system for MCAs was adopted. This aimed at the dismantling and eventual elimination of positive MCAs. Under the new system for compensatory payments, the strongest currency with the highest revaluation rate (usually the German mark) is used as the basis for calculating the new 'green' rates. The pound sterling is not considered here because it does not participate in the Exchange Rate Mechanism of the European Monetary System. After March 1984 a green central rate was established, replacing the old EMS central rates for calculating MCAs. The green central rate is obtained by multiplying the ECU central rate for a currency by the

TABLE 4.5
National Contributions to the Community's Revenues (ECU millions)

Country	1988 forecast	% Of total revenue
Belgium	1 880	4.4
Denmark	965	2.2
France	9 332	21.7
West Germany	11 677	27.2
Greece	422	1.0
Ireland	328	0.8
Italy	6 771	15.7
Luxembourg	87	0.2
Netherlands	2 775	6.5
Portugal	432	1.0
Spain	3 158	7.3
United Kingdom	5 182	12.0

SOURCE   Eurostat, *Basic Statistics of the Community*, 25th edn (Luxembourg: Office for the Official Publications of the European Communities, 1988).

monetary factor of 1.033651. The creation of a green central rate is usually the equivalent of a 3.4 per cent revaluation of the ECU in the agricultural sector and raises the levies and refunds paid. This all sounds very complicated, which it is! It may make more sense when you have read about the ECU in Chapter 7 on money and Chapter 5 on agriculture.

Another Budget Problem – the Winners and Losers

Some countries are net gainers and some are net losers from the financial transactions of the Community. The gainers tend to keep quiet and hope that their luck continues. They are usually the poorer members such as Greece and Ireland although Italy has frequently been a substantial winner. Portugal is likely to become a net beneficiary. The net contributors or 'losers' have been Germany, the

United Kingdom and usually, France. Germany and France, on the one hand, have usually accepted the 'losses' as a reasonable payment to maintain peace and stability in Europe and as a means of helping economic development in less favoured regions. The United Kingdom, on the other hand, has made loud, continuous, and aggressive complaints about its net contributions. In Mrs Thatcher's words 'we want our money back'. Indeed, the problem of the United Kingdom's contributions persisted so long that it threatened to become the bore of the century, rivalling stories about 'Where is Lord Lucan?'

Fortunately for us the matter was largely resolved following the Fontainebleau summit in June 1984. The leaders agreed that expenditure policy is at the heart of any method of controlling budgetary imbalances. This agreement led to subsequent controls on agricultural spending. They also agreed to a system of correction for excessive budgetary burdens with a specific formula for the United Kingdom. These corrections are deducted from the United Kingdom's share of VAT payments in the year following that for which the correction is made. The repayment, rebate, or correction obviously places a burden on the other members – the cost being shared among them according to their normal VAT share – but it is adjusted to allow Germany's share to move to two-thirds of its VAT share. In other words, Germany bears a disproportionate part of the burden of the United Kingdom's rebates despite the fact that it is the largest net contributor (loser) to the Community. Table 4.6 gives figures of estimates from the 1987 budget.

It became apparent very soon after the United Kingdom's accession to the Community that there was likely to be a growing problem of excess budgetary contributions. Denmark, in contrast, was a major net beneficiary. The United Kingdom wanted a closer relationship between payments and receipts. Its wishes were partly granted when the terms of entry were renegotiated. In 1975, the European Council agreed on a corrective mechanism which was to apply for an experimental period of seven years until 1983. This financial mechanism was inadequate since the net debit was not removed and the growth in the size of the United Kingdom's net deficit balance continued. By 1979 the situation was extremely bad. In 1980, it was agreed to reduce the net United Kingdom contribution for 1980 and 1981 from an aggregate of 3924 million ECU to 1339 million ECU. This reduction of 2585 million ECU was

TABLE 4.6
Estimates from the 1987 Budget (£m Net Profit or Loss from the EC Budget)

Greece	+ 1 100	Belgium	+ 210
Ireland	+ 700	Luxembourg	+ 210
Italy	+ 490	Portugal	+ 210
Netherlands	+ 490	France	− 280
Denmark	+ 280	UK	− 770
Spain	+ 280	UK (without rebate)	− 2 380
		West Germany	− 2 900

NOTE   The 1988–9 net payment of the UK was £950 million, that is 0.2 per cent of the UK's GDP.
SOURCE   *The Independent*, 23 November 1987, p. 10.

financed by the other members, partly by direct payments to the United Kingdom Treasury and partly by generous extra payments from the Regional Fund. This did not satisfy Mrs Thatcher who wanted a long-term solution and a control on expenditure. There followed several years of wrangling and almost every summit was soured by this until the 1984 Fontainebleau summit, as previously mentioned.

Is the Community a Tower of Babel?

The Community of Twelve has nine official languages – English, Danish, Dutch, French, German, Greek, Italian, Portuguese and Spanish. This presents a significant financial burden and a personnel problem. All important meetings have to be provided with facilities for translation out of each of nine languages and into the other eight. In addition, all the documents have to be translated into all the official languages. It is estimated that the advent of a new official language created a demand for up to 250 translators. Interpreting into and out of nine languages gives seventy-two potential combinations. This number may be reduced by translating at second hand from a language into which the original language has already been translated. Even then at least thirty translators are needed for nine languages.

There is no chance of the number of official languages being reduced because of political and legal reasons. Formal meetings and documents will, therefore, continue to be available in all nine languages. If Turkey, Norway and Sweden ever join it will be even more like the Tower of Babel. In day-to-day practice, however, the usual working languages of the Community are English and French. The cultural imperialism or encroachment of English is resented and resisted by the French but it is in such a strong position internationally that it is likely to dominate in the long run. Its use by the Americans, the old British dominions and colonies and its adoption by the Japanese and Russians as their second language makes this inevitable. It will be interesting to see, over the next twenty years, what effect satellite broadcasting has on language use. Will it help to perpetuate local languages and dialects through local stations or will it extend English over a wider area?

Agriculture – Too Successful for Its Own Good?

5

Has the Common Agricultural Policy Been Successful?

There is no doubt that the answer to this question is 'yes' *if* the policy is seen in the light of its aims. The critics of the Common Agricultural Policy (CAP) tend to take short-term, oversimplified views. They can see no further than the so-called 'food mountains' and usually feel no need to put forward constructive alternatives to the policies that they wilfully caricature. They condemn the whole policy, in all its complexity, out of hand. What they should be doing is suggesting positive improvements in terms of the CAP's flexibility and ability to respond to changing circumstances.

The CAP was conceived against a history of eighty years of cyclical fluctuations in demand, prices and rural prosperity. Rural poverty in Europe was a mainspring of political and social unrest. The United Kingdom, which tends to take a piously superior attitude to the CAP, was spared much of this because of its earlier shift of resources away from the land into industry. Even so, the agricultural depressions of the 1918–39 period were devastating in the United Kingdom. The stereotype of the Jarrow hunger marchers obscures the reality of this rural deprivation.

The CAP was also founded against the immediate backdrop of over ten years of food shortages in Europe. These were particularly severe from 1943 into the early 1950s, many Europeans dying from malnutrition and its side effects. The foremost aim of the CAP, therefore, was to remove any threat of food shortages. In this the policy has been triumphantly successful.

The other objectives explicitly stated in Article 39 of the Treaty of Rome were: to increase agricultural productivity, to ensure thereby a fair standard of living for the agricultural community, to stabilise markets and to guarantee reasonable prices for consumers.

In order to guarantee food supplies farmers have to be offered secure markets and a fairly high degree of certainty in price levels. This makes some form of state intervention essential. It is the form that this intervention should take that creates division of opinion. Several types of policy are possible and each can be tailored to the specific characteristics of a country. The CAP, covering as it does twelve nations with widely differing climatic conditions, is bound to be less appropriate to some countries than to others. This is not an argument for abolishing it, rather it is a reason for improving its application by fine-tuning to fit national conditions. There is no doubt whatsoever that free competition without state intervention would have resulted in market chaos in Europe with appalling social and economic consequences. It would be flying in the face of all human experience of the last 200 years to advocate free market competition in agriculture.

Why Would Free Market Competition in Agriculture Cause Chaos?

'Chaos' here means successive food gluts and shortages with wide and rapid price fluctuation. It also means cyclical booms and slumps, with concurrent movements in agricultural incomes and employment.

The reasons lie in the nature of agricultural products and their production conditions and in the traditional responses of farmers to changes in markets and prices. These factors, when combined, tend to contradict the simple price theory of elementary economics textbooks, where supply and demand are brought into a neat equilibrium in response to price changes. In agricultural products, there is just as likely to be a series of short-run diverging price equilibria, as shown in the 'cobweb theorem' (see p. 73), and no long-run equilibrium.

Farmers' responses are of paramount importance. There are two main behavioural patterns that can be seen. The first is embodied in what has usually been known as the 'pig cycle', or as the 'hog cycle' in American writings. Pigs are chosen to illustrate this idea because of their ability to reproduce quickly and to be fattened for market in a short time, although there is still a time-lag between planning and achieving production. The same principle now applies to 'lamb' although the cycle is longer and ewes usually have only two lambs a year. It can also apply to arable crops if farmers can quickly enter or leave production. Modern production techniques may cause it to apply to eggs and poultry meat production. The cycle is one of buoyant demand in relation to supply pushing up prices of pig products. Farmers see the high prices and apparent profitability. Existing producers quickly expand their output and newcomers begin production. The result, if demand fails to rise sufficiently, is an excess supply which tends to depress market prices. The fall in price forces marginal producers out of business and reduces profits for the more efficient. The consequent decline in output creates a deficiency of supply in relation to demand. Prices tend to rise and we are back at the starting point. This cycle may take less than two years. Its length, and the range of fluctuation of output and price depends on a number of imponderables such as international price movements, animal feed prices and the movement of the prices of substitutes. Although there may be a similar cycle in some sorts of manufactured goods it is not as intense, partly because many major markets are dominated by oligopolies.

An interesting comparison might be made with the silicon chip market for mass produced chips for electronic devices. These markets have displayed a 'pig cycle' aspect in the 1970s and 1980s. In agricultural markets the 'pig cycle' effect, if unchecked, can destabilise markets and create wider fluctuations in demand, supply and price of products and factors such as labour, transport, animal feed, packaging materials and professional services. It should be remembered, however, that as in all spheres of business some clever entrepreneurs make their profits by anticipating the cycle and bucking the trend. One of the benefits of the CAP has been to remove most of the effects of the cycle in those areas where intervention prices have been applied.

Those readers who are familiar with supply and demand analysis will realise that the above explanation fits the so-called 'cobweb theorem'. This shows how some markets are subject to price destabilisation instead of tending towards an equilibrium. In these conditions the price oscillates around the potential equilibrium but does not settle at it. It may diverge more and more from the equilibrium over time. In diagrams this can be drawn to show a 'cobweb' effect although the 'web' is nowhere near as geometrically accurate as that made by the humble spider! See Figures 5.1 and 5.2.

In principle, then, farmers have always tended to enter markets where prices have been high in the recent past and to leave those where prices have been low. This may be a movement of 'marginal' producers only or may be a shift of a significant proportion of producers. Not all farmers have the luxury of choice as to what to produce. Their land conditions, expertise and machinery may all be specific to one type of production. (There has been a great growth in specialist contracting firms for various types of harvesting. This cuts the costs for farmers entering a new line of production.) In this case, a policy such as the CAP may be used successfully to finance the transfer of land to other uses or to pay farmers to stop producing. The policies adopted need to be flexible and to bear in mind the needs of the individual farmer as well as their effects on aggregate supply.

The second main behavioural pattern of farmers is linked to the first but, to some extent, contradicts it. It consists of farmers, especially those who have a limited range of output options, responding to a fall in their incomes by trying to produce more and to cut their costs. Thus, for example, a typical American Midwest wheat farmer, faced by a falling price of wheat and therefore a falling income, can only compensate by growing more wheat. If all his fellow producers do the same the aggregate supply expands. If demand fails to rise proportionately, excess supply is generated and prices fall even further. This is followed by another fall in net income unless the farmer has managed to cut costs even more. The possible causes of the initial fall in prices and farmers' incomes are many, for example, good harvests in the USSR and elsewhere, or falling real incomes of consumers, or a change in tastes and preferences of consumers. Once again, this response of farmers can be forestalled or controlled by the CAP setting target prices for current and future years and by setting output quotas.

These responses of farmers are partly a reflection of the nature of demand for agricultural products, part of which comes from industry and part from domestic consumers. 'Industrial' demand for the

FIGURE 5.1
'Cobweb' Effects

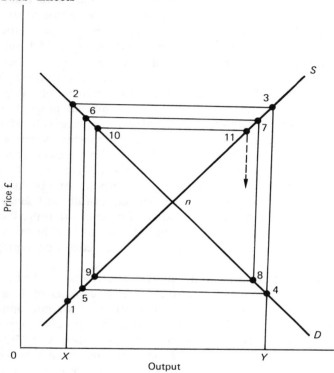

D shows the relationship between the quantity produced in a production period and the price that needs to be charged in order to sell that amount. S shows the relationship between the price in one production period and the quantity that will be produced in the succeeding production period.

If output in period A is OX, the price will be at level 2. The price 2 will cause output in production period B to be OY (point 3) and the price will be at level 4 (where the demand is). Output in production period C will be at level 5 and price at level 6; and so on. Given the relative slopes of these two curves there will be an equilibrium at n. If, however, the curves have a different slope, as in Figure 5.2, this is not the case. Price may diverge further and further from the equilibrium unless the curves shift to a new position.

FIGURE 5.2
'Cobweb' Effects

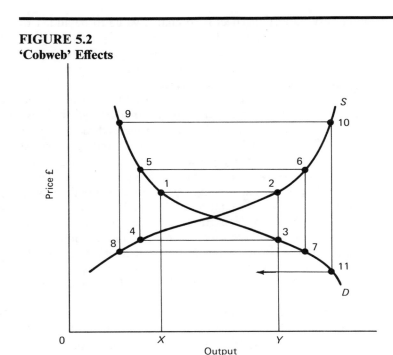

products of agriculture has always been important but modern technology has modified this or provided substitutes via modern chemical processes. The main demands, historically, have been for leather, wool, cotton, other fibres such as flax, dyes, alcohol, starch, oils from seeds, timber and products for brewing. Related to these uses is the manufactured food processing industry which cans, packages and bottles products after dehydration, freezing, pickling, and smoking as a means of preserving the food. Food processing has several effects of great importance to agriculture. Preservation, in itself, can help to smooth out seasonal fluctuations in supply. It can, together with rapid modern transport systems with specialised carriers, make available all sorts of products from all over the world throughout the year, and provides the consumer with substitutes and variety. It also enables surpluses to be extended over time and widely distributed around markets.

Another very important effect is to enable value to be added to what are intrinsically cheap products. This partly explains the great growth since the 1920s of packaged, branded foods. The effect on the market has usually been to create oligopolistic conditions with a few major firms each taking a large share of the market within a given country. They may leave a small proportion of the market to be shared among a larger number of much smaller sellers. These smaller producers survive by producing a specialised product to a narrow section of the market or by giving outstanding personal service or quality. They may enjoy low costs because they are family concerns with fewer overheads. Their continued existence may depend on the larger firms abstaining from trying to take them over because of the threat of investigation under the United Kingdom's Monopolies and Mergers legislation and the Community anti-monopoly laws. Some of the larger firms are multinational and many originate in the USA. There has been a distinct trend towards mergers and marketing arrangements among the dominant firms as the 1992 date for the completion of the single European market approaches.

The processing, packaging and branding of food, together with extensive advertising helps to overcome a basic problem of agriculture in higher income societies. This problem is the existence of a low-income elasticity of demand for some foods and a negative income elasticity for others. Economists give the quaint name of 'inferior goods' to those that have negative income elasticities of demand.

Income elasticity measures the response of the quantity demanded to a change in income. Economists use a formula to measure it:

$$\frac{\text{Income elasticity}}{\text{of demand}} = \frac{\text{Proportionate change in quantity demanded}}{\text{Proportionate change in income}}$$

Theoretically this can vary between minus infinity and plus infinity. Most products show a modest increase in demand as income rises. This gives an income elasticity between zero and unity. Thus income may rise by, say, 5 per cent and the demand for bacon might rise by 2 per cent, giving a measurement of 0.4. Bacon producers could, therefore, expect a slowly expanding demand as society became richer. Many products or services, mainly in the leisure fields, such as sports equipment, restaurant meals or foreign travel show a positive income elasticity above unity. Thus a rise of 5 per cent in income might produce an 8 per cent increase in demand for foreign travel, skis or restaurant meals, giving a measurement of 1.6 per cent. In contrast, there are many foods where a 5 per cent increase in income may be followed by a decrease in demand as people shift their consumption to higher priced, higher protein content, foods. Hence a rise in income of 5 per cent may be followed by a decline in demand for potatoes, sliced white bread, offal and cheaper cuts of meat. The post 1950s' decline in demand for bread and potatoes can be explained in terms of this negative income elasticity of demand. This has had a profound influence on agriculture in terms of incomes and patterns of production. We are, of course, talking in aggregate rather than individual terms and with reference to the United Kingdom and Europe, North America, and higher income countries. In most low-income countries an increase in income is reflected fully in increased demand for basic foodstuffs, but even there a greater proportion of income may be spent on widening the variety of foods consumed.

The nature of the income elasticity of demand for food products in Europe has led to shifts in the pattern of production. There is greater emphasis on meat production of all types, on dairy products and on fruit and horticultural products, while there has been a relative decline in demand for basic arable crops. As will be seen below, the implementation of the CAP has accelerated some of these changes and delayed others. The food processing industry is fully aware of the implications of income elasticity and, with an eye on its profits, has concentrated on products which reflect a higher income elasticity. The relationship between the grower and the food processor has sometimes tended to become one of servant and master. Many farmers have avoided this risk by creating their own cleaning, packaging and branding systems, often in a producers' cooperative.

In terms of conventional price theory, the nature of income elasticity of demand for food means that the demand curve is only slowly shifting to the right as incomes and population increase. Indeed, for individual products, the demand curve may be shifting to the left.

Another major problem for farmers, food processors and policy-makers is that the demand for most foods is price inelastic although the degree of inelasticity differs enormously between products. Price elasticity is a measure of the responsiveness of demand to a small proportionate change in price. A simple formula for measuring it is:

$$\text{Price elasticity of demand} = \frac{\text{Proportionate change in quantity demanded}}{\text{Proportionate change in price}}$$

If the quantity changes proportionately more than the change in price then demand is said to be elastic. This usually means that there are close substitutes at existing market prices.

If the quantity changes less than proportionately compared with the price change then the demand is said to be inelastic. This usually indicates a lack of close substitutes or that the product has a very low price in relation to the average income, or that its purchase is habitual. Looked at from a seller's point of view, an elastic demand means that total revenue (price times quantity sold) from sales will decline as price rises and increase as price falls. Alternatively, an inelastic demand means that his total revenue from sales will increase as price rises and decrease as price falls. These statements are generalisations because price elasticity will, under normal conditions, vary considerably at different price levels. Thus the consequences of agricultural price changes on farmers' revenues will depend, to some extent, on the original price form which the movement occurs. Frequently, a price fall (assuming no state intervention) is the result of increases in supply rather than of any long-term decrease in demand. This creates a tendency to surpluses whose existence exerts a downward pressure on price. If the demand for the farmers' produce is price inelastic the price reduction does not call forth a commensurately larger demand. This is because we have a physical limitation on our consumption of food. There may, however, be a shift in the pattern of consumption. The overall result of increased output and price inelasticity of demand will, therefore, be a reduction in revenues from sales. This does not necessarily mean that profits fall because production costs may have fallen faster than revenues. Often, however, farmers' incomes have fallen in years of good harvests and risen in years of bad harvests. These general points about the effects of relative inelasticity of demand and supply on price can be seen in Figure 5.3.

It is a reasonable conclusion then that a free market in farm products will be a rapidly fluctuating market with periodic shortages and gluts. Prices will be unstable and employment will be uncertain

FIGURE 5.3
Effects of Relative Inelasticity of Demand and Supply on Price

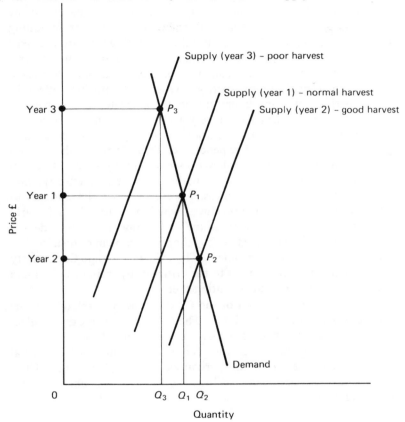

The steep gradient of the curves illustrates the relative inelasticity of supply and demand conditions for this agricultural commodity. Relatively small changes in output produce disproportionately large changes in price.

The figure also illustrates the change in revenue from the sales of this product over the three years. Compare the three rectangles of selling prices multiplied by the quantities OQ_1, OQ_2, OQ_3 in the years 1, 2, and 3.

and there will be a greater risk of political instability. This is borne out by the history of agriculture in pre-intervention days. The destabilising forces are very strong indeed. They are income and price inelasticity of demand (with qualifications), the nature of the 'pig cycle' and the psychological reactions of farmers to falling incomes. It should be borne in mind also that agriculture is a very large consumer of capital goods in the form of buildings, machinery, raw materials and of items such as energy, fuel, and chemicals. Reverses in agricultural prosperity have a severe knock-on effect. In recent periods of rising unemployment, the existence of a healthy farm sector has worked as a very welcome automatic stabiliser, preventing an even greater variation in employment, incomes, and government revenues and expenditure. There is no doubt that an agricultural price support policy is essential in a modern state. On the whole, the CAP has proved to be an extremely effective and efficient policy. Its great weakness, however, has been its tendency to produce surpluses of some products, which has proved particularly undesirable in a world where famine and malnutrition are endemic. It is no good telling people that it is simply a problem of distribution – they see it as a moral problem. The evidence is that Community governments have responded to the criticism by trying to eliminate the surpluses, not by redistributing them.

The other main criticism of the CAP has been in relation to the less developed countries (LDCs). The CAP system of export subsidies has adversely affected the overseas markets of the LDCs, and this has reduced their sales and incomes. In addition, the external tariff around the Community reduces imports from the LDCs, despite various agreements such as the Lomé agreement, aimed at reducing its impact.

Why Have the Surpluses Occurred?

It is obvious that some surplus is usually desirable in order to guard against poor harvests or natural disasters, but by 1987 there were unacceptably large quantities of several products in store in the Community. By 1989, several of these excessive surpluses had been eliminated. The main products in surplus were grains of various kinds, especially wheat and barley, beef, dairy products such as butter and skimmed milk powder, wine and vegetable oils. These stores of produce were very expensive to maintain and were sometimes disposed of in controversial ways, such as in sales of butter to the USSR at very low prices, or in the cheap distribution of beef and butter to pensioners or institutions. In financial terms the surpluses were a great drain on resources and imposed an excessive burden on the consumer. The impact varied from country to country. The seemingly bottomless pit of expenditure on agricultural support was the cause of most of the budgetary problems of the Community. Once the nettle of controlling agricultural price support was grasped, however, the budget problem altered. Indeed, in 1988–9 the Community moved into a budget surplus for the first time. Figure 5.4 shows the principle behind the operation of stock purchases and sales. These are frequently called 'buffer' stocks.

The main cause of the ever growing surpluses lay in the method of setting prices for products. This method varied between products but usually involved setting a target price which would provide a reasonable return for the farmer in an area where the product was a marginal one – that is, where in some years profits were made and in others losses. The idea was to keep such marginal producers in being by giving them a market price that was certain. In order to achieve something like this target price it was necessary to fix an intervention price which was effectively a floor price, somewhere near, but below, the target price. If the producer could not obtain a price better than the intervention price he could sell his product, if its quality were acceptable, to an intervention board at the intervention price. The board would then store the product and hope to release it onto the market if the market price ever rose above the target price. In theory, therefore, prices would not normally ever fall below the intervention price or rise above the target price for long.

There were, in addition, various rebates or subsidies to exports of some food. There was also an external tariff or levy which, according to a complex sliding scale, 'taxed' imports in order to raise their price to prevailing market levels or above. Since the United Kingdom remains a larger importer of food than its fellow members of the Community, particularly of American hard wheat, it appeared to contribute excessively to these levies. The general effect of the pricing system was, and is, to place the burden of agricultural support on the consumer in the form of higher prices. This, it may be argued, is not good in terms of the high burden on lower income groups.

FIGURE 5.4
A Simplified Illustration of a 'Buffer Stock' System in Operation

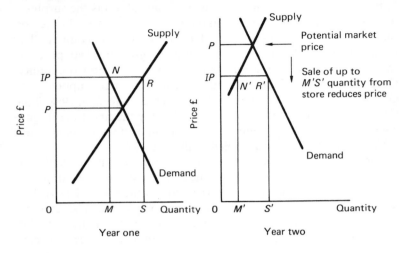

Year one   Year two

Year One
Supply exceeds demand at the proposed intervention price (*IP*) so the market price would settle at *P* which is below the intervention price *IP* guaranteed to the producer by the government, EC, or commodity agreement. The relevant authority buys up enough of the surplus to keep the price up to *IP*. This 'costs' the rectangle *MNRS*, that is the price *IP* times the amount bought, *MS*. Effective demand at the price *IP* is being created by the purchases.

Year Two or some future year
Demand exceeds supply at the intervention price (*IP*), perhaps because of a poor harvest. Thus the free market price (*OP*) without intervention would be above the price guaranteed to the producer, so the authority releases quantities of the product from store. Releasing the quantity *M'S'* would keep the price down to the intervention price. Releasing a smaller quantity would create a price around the target price for the commodity.

NB The CAP intervention system has a target price above the intervention price which is based on producers' costs. The intervention price is, therefore, a 'floor' price which the producer is certain of getting *if* his product is of the correct quality.

The detail of the price support system differs enormously from product to product. These details, and the way in which the regulations are interpreted by the Community bureaucracy and by national governments, matter a very great deal to the individual producer. Until 1987–8, however, the general effect, in which we are interested, was to encourage marginal farmers to continue in production on a regular basis. This was the intention and has helped to maintain prosperity in some regions. The other general effect has been to encourage non-marginal farmers to produce more and for the most efficient to invest large capital sums in expanding output. For many of these farmers the intervention price guaranteed a very healthy profit per unit of output. In pursuit of profit maximisation, they did all the things which now outrage conservationists and created joy among the manufacturers of machinery, chemicals and fertilisers. Banks joined in the fun by lending large quantities of money to farmers. Their lending was safe because of the guaranteed prices of the products. The ownership of land became a desirable investment for institutions such as pensions funds because high agricultural prices enable farmers to pay high rents for leased land. This is Ricardo's theory of rent in operation. To quote the old examination question 'rent is price determined' (see Figure 5.5).

The quest for higher profits from the expansion of output has been accompanied by technological changes which have also generated extra output. These changes have taken many forms. There have been outstanding improvements in productivity from new varieties of arable crops, from the introduction of new breeds of animals and from the adoption of better techniques of animal husbandry. There have also been new fertilisers, better pesticides, improved veterinary practices and medicines. All this has been accompanied by larger, quicker, more versatile and more specialised machinery. There have been notable improvements in buildings and plant as well. The costs of applying these new methods and equipment have been a spur to the creation of larger farm holdings.

The EAGGF

The European Agricultural Guidance and Guarantee Fund (EAGGF) is divided into two parts. The Guarantee part creates the market and price structures needed to maintain and raise farmers'

FIGURE 5.5
Rent is Price Determined

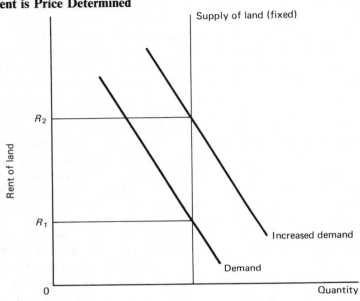

The demand for the product of the land determines the rent paid for the land if it is assumed that land is fixed in supply. If the demand for the product grown on the land, and therefore the product's price, rises then the rent of the land will also rise. The assumption is that the land user can afford to pay more for the land when prices are higher. This assumes that costs remain the same or rise less than the rise in price of the product. It should be remembered that the demand for land is what economists call a 'derived demand', that is to say, it is derived from the demand for the product of the land whether it be turnips, wheat or office space.

incomes. The Guidance section, which has undergone several transformations since it began, is aimed at financing the restructuring of agriculture and helping the less favoured regions. The fund usually provides about 25 per cent of the cost with the remainder coming from the national governments. It has had most impact in France and Germany but will have increasing impact in the newer member countries such as Portugal and Greece. The trend towards larger holdings has been encouraged by this Guidance part of the CAP. It has given financial rewards to hundreds of thousands of small farmers as an encouragement to leave the industry or to alter their production patterns. The land of those giving up farming has usually been swallowed up into larger holdings. The trend to greater output has also been helped by direct subsidies from governments to farmers who wish to drain, plough, build, improve and modernise fields and buildings.

The nature and extent of these improvement grants has altered considerably over the years depending on what the government and Commission see as priorities. One of their main uses has been to give direct financial assistance to special cases such as hill farmers. In their very nature, however, many of them are also available to big 'agri-businesses'. In the United Kingdom, such grants are partly responsible for the disappearance of traditional meadowland, the ploughing of downland, the grubbing up of hedges, the reclamation of moorland, the drainage of wetlands and the sprouting of industrialised farm buildings. An alternative viewpoint is that they have helped to keep the hill farmer in place, thus maintaining the essential character of what is, in reality, a man-made landscape. They have, it is argued, contributed to the maintenance of the economic and social quality of life in the hills and border lands.

Other Reasons for Oversupply

Oversupply sometimes originates in the close production relationships of products or in what economists call 'joint-supply'. There is, for example, a direct relationship between an increased demand for dairy products such as butter, cheeses, cream and yoghurt, and the output of skimmed milk and beef. As incomes and population rise there is a greater demand for dairy products. Therefore, more milk must be produced. This can be achieved up to a point by feeding cows with better food (adding to costs) and by improved technical efficiency. But it can also be done by keeping more cows which will normally have a calf each year in order to maintain their milking capacity and to produce a valuable 'by-product'. The extra calves are either kept as future milking cows, or for beef, or slaughtered for veal, depending on their breeding sire. In practice, of course, a mixture of improved productivity and an increased number of cows is employed. The end result of the attempt to produce more milk for dairy products is the probable output of more beef, although this may not be a problem if the increased population and income also create a greater demand for beef products. It does, however, present problems for farmers who need to feed, house and market the beef cattle because this requires land for growing feed, and, probably, an increased import of animal feed. An alternative policy is the early slaughtering of animals but this tends to reduce their market value and may present problems to the intervention boards. This argument can have a different line if one starts from a situation of an increased demand for beef, which may then create excess milk production, depending on how the industry reacts in using the milk of the cows which bear the calves.

Most of the above discussion about the causes of overproduction has been in the context of traditional northern European products such as grain, meat and dairy produce. There has also been a major difficulty with products such as wine, olive oil and vegetable oils and some fruit and horticultural output.

How Have the Surpluses Been Dealt With?

Initially the surpluses were no real worry since they acted as a traditional buffer stock against future shortages. It was, and remains sensible, to have some surplus. The surplus of output over consumption of cereals, excluding rice, began in 1980–1. It became excessive in 1982–3, declined in 1983–4 and became exorbitantly high in 1984–5, but since then has been controlled to reasonable levels. Butter surpluses of output over consumption began in 1975–6 and reached a peak in 1983. This coincided with a peak yield for dairy cows and a low level of consumption as diet-conscious and unemployed people shifted their purchases to non-milk fats. The actual stocks in intervention stores did not move exactly in line with excess output. They reached a peak in 1986. The wine lake has grown steadily as output has expanded and consumption of ordinary wine has declined. Consumption of wine in Europe fell from 134 million hectolitres in 1976 to 115 million in 1985.

The methods of dealing with surpluses varied with the product but some general attempts were made. There was, for example, the belief that paying small farmers to give up farming would reduce the output of some food, especially in France and West Germany. It did sometimes have this effect but the long-term result was often to increase output, as land which had been inefficiently farmed came into the hands of larger, more efficient farmers. As self-sufficiency has been achieved in some products another general approach has been to encourage the export of food by the use of rebates. These are of immense complexity and have caused much international disquiet. The USA usually regards them as a breach of the General Agreement on Tariffs and Trade. Countries such as Australia and New Zealand see them as creating unfair competition for their products in markets such as Japan. Development economists attack them for creating unfair competition for indigenous producers in developing countries. They are also, allegedly, a gold-mine for fiddlers, twisters and cheats of all descriptions, or for those who understand and can exploit loopholes in the regulations.

Another method adopted to cut the amounts in intervention stores has been the direct sale, in large quantities, of products such as beef, butter and sugar to the Soviet Union. The prices obtained for these bulk sales have often been exceptionally low. They are items which are supposed to have been close to the end of their storage life and any revenue is regarded as beneficial, as is the reduced cost of storage. These sales are politically unpopular. Akin to them are 'gifts' of food to famine-stricken countries. The gift of skimmed milk to impoverished people has been criticised on the grounds that it is harmful to young children because it lacks essential nutrients and requires hygienic preparation. This, it is said, is not always emphasised or possible.

One major device for using intervention stocks has been to make them available to institutions at low prices. These include hospitals, residential homes, and higher education establishments. The assumption is that the demand for these products in the normal, high priced market, is not affected by the offer of low prices for bulk purchase to these bodies. In effect, the intervention board is taking advantage of the differing price elasticities of demand in the two markets – that is the higher elasticity in the institutional market. This is a form of price discrimination. Similar schemes have been aimed at pensioners in distributing beef and butter. An unusual version of this made cheap butter available to all consumers for a short period in 1987. All these schemes have to be used very carefully in order not to destroy the existing orderly market for the product.

The methods mentioned so far failed to attack the basic problem of overproduction and its causes. There was a marked reluctance to tackle the issue by reducing target and intervention prices because of the political ramifications. It would probably not have cut output very much because of the tendency, explained above, of farmers raising output as prices fall in order to maintain their income levels. The most effective technique, therefore, was to impose quotas on output. A quota is a fixed, legally enforceable limit on the output of a product from each production unit. Quotas were applied to milk in 1984 and they were strengthened in 1986. Despite the enormous political furore and the great hardship imposed in an arbitrary fashion on many farmers, the quotas have been very successful. United Kingdom farmers felt particularly ill used, with some justification, because they were the most efficient. Thousands of dairy farmers have gone out of production and the milk quota has become a saleable and transferable financial asset. The quota system, accompanied by 'fines' for overproduction, and a gradually imposed price restraint, has removed most of the milk product surpluses. There is still room for some improvement in the system to make it fairer and less arbitrary.

The methods used to cut surpluses of grain have also been successful. They began with a 'coresponsibility levy' on output. This is, in effect, a tax on output and is therefore in direct conflict with the price support principles of the CAP. It has been varied and falls most heavily on large-scale producers. Then an upper limit was placed on the total output quantity on which the intervention prices were payable. (This was similar to the United Kingdom system that existed before 1972. That limited the financial commitment of the government to a certain preordained volume of output.) Beyond this quantity the producers have no guaranteed price or sale. The checks on quality were tightened so that intervention prices are now more related to quality.

Thus, with milk and cereals, the Community has managed to get away from the stranglehold of unrestricted price guarantees. It can now limit the guarantee to a predetermined amount and can affect the price received by the farmer by 'fines' and 'coresponsibility levies'.

Several other minor attempts at dissolving surpluses have been made. Some of them have been marginally effective. Others have been ludicrously expensive to implement. For example, wine growers have been paid to destroy vines. This has been worthwhile. One scheme which turned excess wine into industrial alcohol and another to turn butter into a condensed cooking fat, were extremely expensive. Yet another scheme ended up feeding surplus milk products back to cattle.

Eventually, in 1986, the Community adopted a version of a policy that was first adopted in the USA in the 1930s, which consisted of paying farmers to leave land fallow. The European scheme is called 'set-aside' and is more complicated, sophisticated or cumbersome according to your viewpoint. In return for a cash payment per year, a farmer undertakes to remove a percentage of his land from the cultivation of certain arable crops. This policy is accompanied by inducements for what is called 'extensification', broadening the use of land into a greater variety of crops and into non-agricultural uses. The environmental lobby has high hopes that set-aside will be a stimulus to reafforestation with broad-leaved trees and to the establishment of new footpaths, bridleways and recreational areas. However, American experience does not give much cause for optimism about the effectiveness of set-aside. In that case there were massive improvements in productivity from the land that remained in cultivation, but the result was that overproduction reappeared. In the United Kingdom, the risk of this happening has been somewhat reduced by the removal of fertiliser subsidies and various land improvement grants. The diversification of land use and employment in rural areas in the United Kingdom will be gradually extended because there has been a relaxation of planning controls on the use of agricultural buildings. It is hoped that old buildings will be converted for small enterprises and workshops. Tourist boards and enterprise agencies are also encouraging a diversification of farm activities.

All these policies, taken together, have been effective in removing the excessively large intervention stocks. Consequently, the financial burden of the CAP has been lightened and the Community budget was in surplus in 1988–9. It remains to be seen whether these policies can be sustained because, for example, farm incomes in the United Kingdom fell by 40 per cent in 1988–9. The main reasons for this were the 'low' levels set for target prices and the rise in production costs. Farmers are a particularly strong political lobby, especially in mainland Europe. It is unlikely that they will meekly accept a permanent reduction in their standard of living. Having said that, the number of people engaged in agriculture has steadily declined over the last twenty years and the lobbies which have interests in opposition to the farmers have been growing in strength and influence.

What of the Future?

Demographic trends do not bode well for European agriculture. The population of the Community is expected to rise by 2 per cent from 1985 to 2005. The populations of West Germany and Belgium are expected to fall. There may be extra growth in world markets because the world population is predicted to grow by 36 per cent in the same period. It is reasonable to expect, therefore, that within the European Community there will be little expansion of total consumption of staples such as wheat for flour, potatoes and bulk vegetables. Patterns of consumption will continue to change if real incomes rise as anticipated. Allowing for fashions in diet, there will be a continued shift of demand to meat products, dairy products and higher quality fruit, vegetables and horticultural products. Land use will respond to the need to feed more animals.

In some areas, there will be a return to mixed farming and a shift away from monoculture. There is also likely to be an extension of afforestation and more land will be dedicated to recreational use of various sorts, including nature conservation areas. Moreover, there will be a continued drain of land into building development for housing and industry. This will be harder to oppose if the required level of food production can be achieved with a smaller area of land in cultivation. Some farmers will apply the benefits of the latest biotechnological developments in plant types, animal breeding and recycling of materials.

In the future, there are likely to be two conflicting trends. On the one hand, there will be pressure to produce standardised, quality controlled products for a mass market. This will be assisted by established grading and packaging standards which will be extended under the single European market. On the other hand, there will be a growing market for high quality, organically produced food from those who are able to pay the inevitably higher prices. It is in this sphere that the smaller, more localised producer will flourish. However, all these predictions will be invalidated if there is a major shift in climatic conditions over the next twenty years.

Economic Performance 6

Introduction

The measurement of economic performance is notoriously difficult and fraught with controversy. The comparison of the economic performance of two or more countries or trading blocs is even more problematical. When it is eventually agreed what to measure and with what units, there may still be disagreement about the relative merits of various aspects of performance. An analogy of the problem may be seen in the task of a motoring correspondent who has to draw up a comparison of a mini and a high performance sports car. You can measure, fairly objectively, top speed, acceleration, petrol consumption, luggage room, seats and maintenance costs, but many of these are dependent upon the operating context – urban, rural or motorway. A traffic jam on the M25 reduces them to temporary equality in most respects except the comfort of the seats and the quality of the 'in car entertainment'. Similarly, two or more economies can be compared objectively but only up to a point. The context of the comparison and the base from which it is made then becomes of paramount importance.

Much of the emphasis of comparison of economic performance is upon rates of growth of various indices or absolute quantity. The implicit assumption is that all growth is good and that higher growth is better. This is, of course, nonsense because the costs of the growth to society may be excessive. It may reduce welfare, increase ill health, raise death rates and exploit Third World countries. The growth may also be very unevenly distributed. The present fashion for market driven economies tends to ignore these facts. Part of the argument about the policies to be implemented to achieve the single market is really about distribution of growth, although the main emphasis is on overall growth. President Mitterrand of France and Jacques Delors, President of the Commission, are both quoted as not wanting a Europe for bankers only but for workers as well.

Having expressed all these doubts it remains necessary to attempt some assessment of relative economic performance. We should, however, bear in mind that we cannot know what might have happened if the United Kingdom, or indeed other members, had not joined the Community. We should also remember, when making comparisons, that the Community only partially determines or influences the environment in which it operates. Changes in the international trade cycle, international interest rates and in other countries' economic policies are beyond its control. So too are natural disasters, international conflicts and political upheavals. An added factor is the need to make allowances for foreign exchange rates and their movements.

What Measures of Comparison Are Useful?

Almost all international, and for that matter national, comparison starts from the calculation of Gross Domestic Product – that is, from national income statistics. The United Nations has a preferred method for this calculation and one of the best sources of data is the annual *Statistical Yearbook*. Some nations, including the United Kingdom, do not adhere strictly to this method. In Britain's case, it does not put a monetary figure on the value of housewives' services.

This is not the place for a full description of national income accounting, but a brief explanation is needed. When measuring the national income the economist is calculating the amount of money income obtained by the nation in the form of wages, salaries and so on, profits and rent, in return for producing consumer goods and services, investment goods and public goods. By definition, allowing for the niceties of the calculation, national income should equal the value added to the national output. In measuring the national output it is important to avoid 'double counting' of items and to measure only the value added at each stage of production. Also by definition, the national income equals the amount of money spent on the purchase of capital and consumption goods. In this third method of calculation which is called the 'expenditure method', care has to be taken to avoid double or miscounting, especially with respect to indirect taxation and subsidies. There is a 'factor cost adjustment' to take care of this. The statistics can be related to the domestic stage only or can be modified to allow for foreign payments, income and expenditure. The phrase 'national' is then applied to the statistics as in statements such as 'national income = national expenditure = national output'. A final adjustment is made to allow for capital consumption or depreciation because output undertaken simply to replace worn out equipment is not a net addition to output. This calculation, deducting a figure for capital consumption, turns the figures from 'gross' to 'net'. The figures used for this item of capital consumption are estimates and are among the least reliable of the national income statistics. At the end of all this, the economist concludes that national income = national expenditure = net national product (national output).

What then have we got as a basis of comparison? We have a fairly accurate measure of the value of new output in a year, of the income derived from producing it, and of its monetary value in terms of expenditure. If we then wish to compare changes over time we need to make allowances for changes in price levels. This is done by taking a base year and using a price index as a 'deflator'. For example, in order to compare the national income of 1989 with that of 1979 we need to use, say, 1979 price levels for both and convert the 1989 figures by the amount by which an index of general prices has risen over the ten years. This is called converting money national income into 'real' national income. It simply means that account has been taken of inflation. It is also necessary, sometimes, to take notice of movements in the level of population over time and to calculate money or real national income per head. This is only a rough guide to living standards and it is best to combine it with an analysis of the distribution of income per head, although these figures are among the least reliable of all those available. They are also capable of many different interpretations.

Other useful statistics for international comparison are crude output statistics or changes in them as measured by an index, and levels of possession of standard consumer durable goods such as telephones, video recorders or television sets per head. Interesting results can be obtained from studying how many minutes or hours an average worker must work to be able to buy standard goods or services such as a kilo of butter, a unit of electricity, a small car or a loaf of bread. Other statistics which are valuable for comparative studies are those of working hours, average earnings and productivity.

These then are some of the basic measurements of comparison. If we take account of all the warnings about their validity and usefulness, how has the European Community fared?

How Has the Community Performed?

The two sets of figures given in Tables 6.1 and 6.2 are a rough measure of how living standards have changed. The first set measures Gross Domestic Product per head. The figures are at current prices and at what are called 'purchasing power parities'. These take account of exchange rate differences and are far too complex to explain in this context. Suffice it to say, most economists think they are the best way of coping with changes in foreign exchange rates over time when using statistics. They should be considered in conjunction with the second set which gives figures of Volume Indices of GDP at market prices.

A mass of statistics such as Tables 6.1 and 6.2 is capable of many interpretations or variations of emphasis. The figures for Turkey and Austria have been included because they are potential entrants to the Community, and because the Austrian economy has sometimes been held up as something to be emulated. It is clear that Turkey's economic position is well behind that of even the poorer members of the Community such as Portugal, Ireland or Greece, although its recent growth rate has been exceptionally high. Norway has been included because it decided, by referendum, not to join the Community when the United Kingdom did. Norway remained part of EFTA which has developed very close trading links with the Community. It benefited from oil and gas discoveries at the same time as the United Kingdom but has made much better use of its oil revenues to restructure its economy. Norway is currently reconsidering applying for membership of the Community. It is interesting to compare growth rates. The figures in Table 6.3 are at constant prices and, therefore, make allowances for inflation.

TABLE 6.1

Gross Domestic Product at Market Prices Per Head (at Current Prices and Purchasing Power Parities) (ECU)

Country	1981	1986
Europe 12	8 770	13 639
USA	13 591	21 307
Japan	9 194	15 155
UK	8 764	14 158
Belgium	9 041	13 883
Denmark	9 535	16 025
West Germany	10 033	15 702
Greece	5 090	7 670
Spain	6 392	9 893
France	9 900	15 042
Ireland	5 808	8 537
Italy	9 042	14 037
Luxembourg	10 258	17 326
Netherlands	9 673	14 527
Portugal	4 775	7 196
Turkey	1 310	1 404
Norway	14 473	20 612
Austria	9 110	15 252

SOURCE   For Tables 6.1, 6.2, 6.3: Eurostat, *Basic Statistics of the Community*, 25th edn (Luxembourg: Office for Official Publications of the European Communities, 1988).

It can be seen that the growth performance of the European Twelve between 1981 and 1986 was inferior to that of both the United States and Japan, and that the United Kingdom was among the better performers in the Community. The United Kingdom's performance should perhaps be compared with Norway's, in that both were affected by oil revenues from the North Sea. It should also be seen against the rapid deindustrialisation of the early 1980s when British manufacturing industry suffered a devastating decline. It would have been reasonable to expect that the enormous revenues from North Sea oil would have been used to renovate and re-equip

TABLE 6.2
Volume Indices (1980 = 100; GDP at Market Prices)

Country	1981	1986
Europe 12	100.2	110.3
USA	103.7	119.6
Japan	103.9	123.9
UK	98.8	112.6
Belgium	98.6	106.2
Denmark	99.1	116.7
West Germany	100.2	108.8
Greece	100.1	108.1
Spain	99.8	110.6
France	101.2	110.0
Ireland	103.3	109.3
Italy	101.1	111.3
Luxembourg	99.8	118.6
Netherlands	99.3	107.3
Portugal	101.3	109.6
Turkey	104.4	136.7
Norway	100.9	123.2
Austria	99.9	109.3

British industry. One cannot imagine the Japanese missing such an opportunity. Instead it appears that the advantage has been used to finance social security for the unemployed or, if you look at it differently, on investment overseas. The long-term opportunity cost of such a policy, or absence of policy, will be immense.

The causes of economic growth are not always easily identifiable or quantifiable, nor is the relative emphasis to be given to each. It is usually agreed, however, that investment expenditure, the application of new technology, research and development expenditure, improved education and training of the population, and the shift of workers from less productive to more productive employment are important determinants of the rate of growth of GDP. In recent years, more emphasis has been placed on the detailed nature of the

TABLE 6.3

Annual Rates of Growth of GDP at Market Prices (At Constant Prices, 1981–6)

Country	Total	Per Head of Total Population	Per Head of Occupied Population
Europe 12	1.9	1.7	1.9
USA	2.9	1.9	1.2
Japan	3.6	2.9	2.7
UK	2.6	2.5	2.5
Belgium	1.5	1.5	1.6
Denmark	3.3	3.3	1.9
West Germany	1.7	1.9	2.0
Greece	1.6	1.1	1.2
Spain	2.1	1.6	2.8
France	1.7	1.2	1.9
Ireland	1.1	0.6	2.8
Italy	1.9	1.7	1.1
Luxembourg	1.6	3.4	2.7
Netherlands	1.6	1.1	1.8
Portugal	1.6	1.1	2.7
Turkey	5.5	3.3	n.a.
Norway	4.1	3.7	n.a.
Austria	1.8	1.8	n.a.

research and development (R & D) expenditure. Japan spends a relatively small proportion of its R & D money on defence associated uses; the United Kingdom and the United States spend a relatively high percentage. The available evidence seems to demonstrate conclusively that Japan benefits greatly from her policy and that the United Kingdom suffers from hers.

The United Kingdom government has produced sets of statistics emphasising the great improvement in the country's economic performance in the 1980s compared with previous decades. The figures are mainly based on productivity growth per person employed. These statistics, as presented, are impressive but are the subject of continuing debate among economists about their validity and relevance. For example, they usually take 1980 or 1981 as their starting base and measure changes rather than the absolute figures for output, so that they discount the drop in manufacturing output in the early 1980s. If they are taken in the context of the general use of statistics by the government since 1979, then they need to be treated with great caution. The government has consistently manipulated the unemployment figures in order to reduce the recorded number. It has also indulged in what some people see as odd accounting practices with regard to the sales of nationalised industry assets, counting the proceeds as negative expenditure. The government use of statistics on the National Health Service is also highly suspect – it is probably safer to use *Eurostat* figures. However, some of the relevant figures are given in Tables 6.4 and 6.5, 6.6 and 6.7.

TABLE 6.4
Output Per Person Employed – Whole Economy (Average Annual % Changes)

	1960–70	*1970–80*	*1980–88*
UK	2.4	1.3	2.5
US	2.0	0.4	1.2
Japan	8.9	3.8	2.9
West Germany	4.4	2.8	1.8
France	4.6	2.8	2.0
Italy	6.3	2.6	2.0
Canada	2.4	1.5	1.4
G7 average	3.5	1.7	1.8

UK data from Central Statistical office. Other countries' data from OECD except 1988 which are calculated from national GNP or GDP figures and OECD employment estimates.

SOURCE   For Tables 6.4, 6.5, 6.6, 6.7: 'Economic Progress Report No. 201', April (London: HM Treasury/HMSO, 1989).

TABLE 6.5
Output Per Person Employed – Manufacturing Industry (Average Annual % Changes)

	1960–70	*1970–80*	*1980–88*
UK	3.0	1.6	5.2
US	3.5	3.0	4.0
Japan	8.8	5.3	3.1
West Germany	4.1	2.9	2.2
France	5.4	3.2	3.1
Italy	5.4	3.0	3.5
Canada	3.4	3.0	3.6
G7 average	4.5	3.3	3.6

UK data from Central Statistical office. Other countries' data from OECD except France and Italy which use IMF employment data. 1988 data for France and Italy cover first three quarters only.

What Have Been the Longer Term Trends?

Over the twenty-five years from 1960 the GDP per head in Europe doubled. In contrast, that in Japan quadrupled. In the United States, it grew by 60 per cent. In absolute terms, in 1985, the USA's GDP per head was 56 per cent higher than Europe's; Japan's was 11 per cent higher. In general, the more mature economies of Europe such as the United Kingdom (average annual growth rate 2.2 per cent 1960–85) grew more slowly than the less mature such as Spain (4.6 per cent) and Portugal (5.1 per cent).

In terms of total output the United States still dominates. In 1985, the United States' GDP, in thousand million ECUs, was 5172, the Community of Twelve's was 3314, and Japan's 1754. These average figures hide wide regional disparities within the individual nations. The broad national differences can be seen in the tables of GDP per head. The alleged North–South divide in the United Kingdom is one obvious example of the regional variations in income, employment and other variables used to measure the quality of life.

TABLE 6.6
Relative Productivity Levels (Whole Economy 1986)

	GDP Per Head of Population	GDP Per Person Employed	GDP Per Hour Worked
UK	100	100	100
US	150	141	132
Japan	106	94	67
West Germany	110	113	105
France	106	119	117
Italy	100		
Canada	140	131	116

Average annual hours worked per person employed supplied by A. Maddison, calculated as in appendix C of his *Phases of Capitalist Development* (1982).
Figures for Italy incomplete because of uncertainties in the size of the hidden economy.

TABLE 6.7
Employment and Hours Worked, 1986

	% of Population in Employment	Average Annual Hours Worked Per Person Employed
UK	43.0	1511
US	45.4	1609
Japan	48.2	2129
West Germany	41.4	1630
France	37.8	1533
Canada	45.9	1704

In the future, longer term, it is expected that changes involved in creating a genuine single market up to 1992 and beyond will be a major stimulus to economic growth. Labour and capital should be more mobile and the costs of production and movement of goods should be significantly lower.

Employment Comparisons

Since 1975 both the United States and Japan have coped much more effectively with unemployment than Europe. The figures given in Table 6.8 show this clearly. We have to assume that 'unemployment' means the same thing in each area.

The European statistics represent an average of a very wide range of unemployment in the member states. In 1986, the unemployment rates as a percentage of civilian working population were:

Belgium	12.5	Ireland	18.3
Denmark	7.4	Italy	13.7
West Germany	8.1	Luxembourg	1.5
Greece	7.4	Netherlands	12.4
Spain	21.2	Portugal	8.8
France	10.7	UK	12.0
			(est.)

TABLE 6.8
Unemployment Rate (%)

	Europe 12	*Japan*	*United States*
1975	2.9	1.9	8.5
1981	7.8	2.2	7.6
1985	10.6	2.6	7.2
1986	10.7	2.8	7.0

SOURCE Eurostat, *Basic Statistics of the Community*, 25th edn (Luxembourg: Office for Official Publications of the European Communities, 1988).

A particularly worrying aspect of the unemployment figures is the high proportion of the unemployed who are under 25 and the growing incidence of long-term unemployment. In April 1986, for example, in the Twelve, 41 per cent of all unemployed persons were under 25, and 52 per cent had been unemployed for more than a year. About a third had been without a job for over two years. Overall about 47 per cent of those without work were women but this average covered a range from 34 per cent in Ireland to 62 per cent in Belgium. The United Kingdom's proportion for female unemployment was 40.4 per cent of the total. In the United Kingdom 35 per cent of the jobless were under 25.

Some economists and politicians prefer the emphasis to be placed on job creation rates rather than on unemployment. There is an increasing amount of literature analysing the number and type of jobs created over recent years in both the United States and Europe. The conclusions from the research are often ambiguous or even contradictory. The interpretation of such studies may result in value judgements about the new jobs in the tertiary sector, especially in personal services, as being 'inferior' to the lost jobs in manufacturing industry. The new jobs may be part time, seasonal, low wage and unskilled. The best test of whether such job creation is satisfactory is to look at the skill and experience of the remaining unemployed and see whether it is matched to any extent by the nature of vacant jobs. It may be that there has been a long-term structural decline in an industry, as in coal mining. This means that few relevant new jobs will appear and that retraining is the only solution to the problem. This retraining has been the role of the Social Fund and Regional Development Funds of the Community.

The Community's role with respect to unemployment generally has been peripheral because it is regarded as a function of national governments to control their own internal economies and thus their own levels of unemployment.

The Service Sector

The service, or tertiary, sector consists of commerce, transport, banking, insurance, administration, distribution and personal services. In the Community, in 1975, about 60 million people were engaged in the tertiary sector. This was about 49 per cent of the total civilian labour force. By 1985 the percentage had risen to 58 per cent. In the same period, 1975 to 1985, the share of the sector in the GDP rose from 47 to 57 per cent. These changes may appear rapid but they were even more pronounced in Japan and the United States. Employment in the tertiary sector rose by 17 per cent compared with about 20 per cent in Japan and 32 per cent in the United States. The growth of this sector is often seen as a major sign of an economy moving into a post-industrial phase. This is something of an oversimplification because some undeveloped economies have large personal service employment simply because labour is exceptionally cheap. They do not, however, have large employment in banking and financial services.

Many of the manufacturing jobs have been lost through improvements in technology and through transfer to developing countries. The resultant decline of skilled and semi-skilled employment in manufacturing is a cause for concern because there is a limit to which the personal services sector can absorb the unwanted labour. We cannot all survive by taking in each other's washing. Once again, there is a need for a retraining programme to raise the level of workers' skill and mobility.

Trade Comparisons

The Community was formed with the intention of easing and stimulating trade between its members by reducing all barriers between them. The tariff barriers were quickly removed by 1968 and the non-tariff barriers should be removed by the end of 1992. It was also expected that the Community's internal market would expand and enable firms to benefit from the considerable economies of scale available in a market rising to over 320 million relatively affluent people. The cost-reducing benefits from such a large internal market would, it was anticipated, enable Community firms to compete effectively in world markets. The Japanese, by comparison, have a home market of only 120 million, the United States of 240 million and the USSR of 280 million. These promised benefits have never fully materialised but the European Community is, by most standards, the most important trading group in the world. As an importer Europe is slightly less important than the United States but on the export side it was responsible, in 1986, for 19 per cent of world trade compared with the United States' 13 per cent and Japan's 12 per cent.

How has intra-Community trade developed?

Trade between members, intra-Community trade, has grown much faster since 1958 than trade with non-members. Between 1958 and 1986 trade between members increased by 36 times whereas trade with non-members rose 16 times. The pattern varies but for most members intra-Community trade accounts for over half their total trade. The countries most dependent on intra-Community trade are Ireland, Belgium, Luxembourg and the Netherlands. The least dependent is the United Kingdom whose exports to the Community in 1986 were only 47 per cent of her total exports. About half her imports were from the other members. Denmark's figures were very similar to the United Kingdom's. In the case of all the other members more than half their imports came from other members and more than half their exports went to other members. Despite the above figures, the United Kingdom has been increasingly dependent since 1958 on trade with Community members. In 1958, only about 16 per cent of her exports and 20 per cent of her imports arose from trade with the Community.

How has the Community's external trade changed?

There have been major changes over the years in the composition of the imports. Initially, the Community was predominantly an importer of raw materials and processed them into manufactured goods for consumption and export. Gradually the position altered and an increasing proportion of imports has been of semi-finished goods and manufactured articles. Thus, by 1986, more than half the Community's imports were manufactured goods, finished or semi-finished. The United Kingdom's trade has, of course, altered in the same way so that it now has a very large deficit on visible trade in manufactures.

One of the main variables in Community trade has been oil and natural gas. Some of this has been derived from within the Community, that is, from the United Kingdom and Holland, but most is bought on world markets where the price is very volatile. Large quantities of gas are bought from the Soviet Union. In common with other countries the Community's trade volume has altered as oil and energy prices have fluctuated. The heavy reliance upon oil imports pushed the Community's overall visible trade balance into deeper deficit until the large reduction of oil prices occurred in 1985. On visible trade, the Community was in deficit from 1958 until 1986 when a surplus was achieved. The oil price change also had an impact on 'invisible' payments in the form of interest, dividends, profits, and the purchase of financial and transport services.

The changes in the Community's current account balances

A country's balance of payments on current account is made up of two main components. The first is payments for visible imports and exports of goods and is called the 'balance of trade'. The second is called the 'invisible balance' and consists of payments into and out of a country for services and other transfers. The most important of these invisible imports and exports are payments for banking, insurance and other financial services. The other main flow of money is interest, profits and dividends from investments in other countries or paid out to foreigners who have made financial investments in the country. Tourism and travel give rise to large invisible flows and so does the purchase of shipping and air services. There are, in addition, private transfers to or from individuals living in different countries. A country such as the United Kingdom earns large surpluses on its invisible account because of the activities of the financial and commodity markets in London and because of the very large holdings of property and financial investments abroad. This is despite the expansion of foreign holdings of assets in the United Kingdom which create an outflow of interest, profits and dividends each year. It should be noted in this context that, if the United Kingdom's prevailing interest rate levels are high compared with those in other countries, there will tend to be an enlarged flow of foreign capital into the United Kingdom. This will necessitate larger future outflows of interest payments unless the interest is reinvested in Britain.

When the two components, the balance of visible trade and the balance of invisibles, are added together we have the 'balance of payments on current account'. There is also an account kept of movements of capital into and out of a country. These may consist of flows originating from individuals, firms or governments. They may be moved either on a short-term or long-term basis. The transfer of such funds affects the foreign exchange markets.

Visible trade

Each of the twelve members of the Community has its own accounts for visible and invisible trade and therefore an individual balance of payments on current account. These accounts show great variety. In 1986, for example, only West Germany, France, Denmark and Ireland had surpluses in visible trade outside the Community. Of the total surplus of 38 billion ECU of the Twelve, West Germany earned 30 billion. This shows the importance of Germany in the Community. The aggregate trade deficit in trade outside the Community was 33 billion ECU. The Netherlands accounted for 35 per cent of this and the United Kingdom 22 per cent. Overall the extra-Community trade balance was about 5 billion ECU in surplus, that is 38 billion surpluses minus 33 billion deficits.

Invisible trade and current account balances

In 1986, Denmark, Greece, Ireland and the United Kingdom had current account deficits. The United Kingdom had a large invisible surplus but it was not sufficient to match the visible deficit. This visible deficit has continued to widen into 1989. The Community as a whole had moved into current account deficit in 1978–9 and continued in deficit until 1983. Thereafter an increasing surplus has been achieved and reached 49 billion ECU in 1986.

There are major influences on the trend of the current account. The most important are the value of the ECU against the dollar and the yen, and world oil prices. As these change the costs of production of European goods alters and their competitiveness in home and foreign markets is affected. The Japanese have been building up balance of payments on current account surpluses (80 billion ECU in 1986) and the United States has been struggling to reduce its deficit (140 billion ECU in 1986). The changes in these totals and the measures taken to disperse the surplus or reduce the deficit affect interest rates and exchange rates. It can be seen, therefore, that Community trade is partly at the mercy of Japanese and American policies. As a general rule countries with surpluses are reluctant to take swift action to reduce them. Countries in deficit are also slow to take remedial action.

Money 7

What Determines the Value of the Various European Currencies?

A number of factors influence the value of a currency compared with another. These factors change in relative importance over time. They include the supply and demand of the currency in world foreign exchange markets, the extent and nature of official controls on movements of money in or out of a country, government policy and the possible existence of international agreements on foreign exchange rates. An example of this last factor was the Bretton Woods agreement on fixed parities which survived from 1947 to 1971. Another is the European Monetary System (EMS), or more specifically the Exchange Rate Mechanism (ERM) which is part of it.

Economists try to explain the fundamental relationship of two currencies in terms of the 'purchasing power parity' theory (PPP). This formidable title disguises a fairly simple idea, although, needless to say, it can be expressed in a variety of ways and with different degrees of sophistication. At its simplest the theory says that a given collection or 'basket' of goods will have a certain price in each of two countries. This price will, of course, be expressed in the two different currencies. The PPP then says that the foreign exchange rate between the two currencies will tend towards that existing in the prices of the basket of goods in the two countries. So, if our basket costs £20 in the United Kingdom and $30 in the United States, the foreign exchange rate will tend to be around £1 = $1.5. This is

107

because the competitive nature of the markets leads to shifts in the supply and demand for goods and services as price differences become apparent.

How Well Does the Purchasing Power Parity Theory Apply?

This theory seems to show basic common sense and can be seen in operation in cross-border trade between neighbouring underdeveloped countries. It does, however, become less applicable in the short term in developed economies although its long-run applicability remains valid. The PPP theory is much harder to apply when capital as well as goods and services enter into trade and when speculation is rife.

Another major problem which arises is the fact that certain important items of expenditure do not entail trade or international exchange. Such items may be power, such as electricity, housing services, a wide range of personal services and local or central government services. More sophisticated versions of the theory try to take this into account and there is sound evidence that the PPP theory of an exchange rate between two countries is valid over time, albeit with short-term aberrations.

Where Does the Non-speculative Demand and Supply of a Currency Come From?

The demand for the pound, on the one hand, comes from foreigners who wish to buy British exports and need to pay British companies in sterling. This demand arises from both visible exports and invisible exports of services such as tourism, banking, insurance, and so on. Obviously this demand relates to the volume of such trade which, in itself, is affected by comparative rates of inflation. Other things being equal, a high exchange rate for the pound will reduce the demand for the United Kingdom's exports. The extent of the reduction will depend on the price elasticity of demand for the exports. Price elasticity of demand measures the responsiveness of demand to price changes. In effect, within certain exchange rate limits, United Kingdom exports yield greater total revenue as the exchange rate of the pound drops.

The other non-speculative demand for the pound arises when foreign companies and individuals wish to transfer capital to Britain for investment purposes. This may be physical investment in the Keynesian sense of expenditure on capital goods such as factories or plant. It may, however, be the transfer of money capital for deposit in a wide range of short-term or long-term financial assets. This type of monetary flow is influenced by the interest rate levels prevailing within the United Kingdom compared with those in other similar economies. They also respond to changes in the comparative rates of inflation and to expectations of movements in foreign exchange rates in different countries. The money is used to buy bills of exchange, Treasury Bills, short- and long-dated government stock, local authority bonds, various types of certificates of deposit and company shares.

The United Kingdom has long been a major international financial centre although the pre-eminence of the City of London is fading. As a result of this role there are extremely large flows of capital into and out of sterling. The 'City', meaning the banks and financial institutions, earns large fees and commissions on such transfers. Those paid by foreigners are part of the United Kingdom's invisible earnings on the balance of international payments. Some of these flows into short-dated bills or bonds are very 'liquid', that is convertible into cash, and are transferred easily and quickly, though at some expense, into other currencies if conditions change. These funds which move quickly for very short-term gains are sometimes called 'hot money' – an inescapable element in the foreign exchange markets. It is also frequently an undesirable element.

The supply of pounds, on the other hand, is produced by the reverse elements of the factors described above. That is to say, importers need to sell pounds in order to get the foreign currency required by their overseas suppliers. British tourists are selling pounds to buy the currency they need for their holidays. There is also a large supply of pounds arising from the great volume of investment abroad by British firms and individuals. This investment has, over the years, reached a huge total and economists take an intense interest in its destinations. In recent years, to 1989, North America has been a favourite destination for British overseas investment. Some of this transfer originates in the fashion for take-overs of American firms as a quick way of getting into the North American market.

What Is the Role of Speculation in the Fixing of Exchange Rates?

Most of the currency bought and sold in the foreign exchange markets is dealt in with a speculative profit in mind or with the intention of avoiding loss. That is to say, the buyers and sellers do not want the currency to finance visible or invisible trade or capital movements. They are hoping for a profit after the costs of transfer are met from buying or selling. The simplest form of speculation is to buy in the hope or expectation of the price rising in the future so that a capital gain can be made. A more complicated alternative is to sell, at a high price, something that you do not yet possess in the hope that you can buy it at a lower price in order to meet your obligation to deliver it. Markets vary in the scope that they give speculators to operate.

Speculation is made a normal activity in the foreign exchange markets by the existence, side by side, of a 'spot' market and a 'forward' market. A spot market refers, as its name suggests, to a deal based on the current prices prevailing as the deal is fixed. A forward market is often called a 'futures' market when commodities are concerned. It allows dealers to reach agreement on price at one moment on a deal to be concluded in the future – days, weeks or months ahead. The bargain is made. The price to be paid is fixed and must be honoured when the date arrives. Such forward markets do serve a very useful function, enabling buyers and sellers of goods to fix their costs in advance. Thus, for example, an importer of raw materials makes his forward deal so that he can calculate exactly the costs of production arising from the purchase of foreign exchange to pay for the materials.

The existence of forward markets is a great stimulus to speculation but this does not necessarily create greater fluctuation in exchange rates. Indeed, some economists argue that an efficient, well-informed speculative market may iron out the peaks and troughs of foreign exchange rate movements. This will reduce the range of fluctuation because speculators need to take their profits while they can and there are always some who try to get out of a rising market by selling before it peaks. Alternatively, they may buy in a falling market before it bottoms out. By so doing they will, if they do it in sufficient volume, cause the rise to cease or the fall to halt. There is also an activity called 'hedging' which involves a loss of overall profit but ensures a profit or prevents a loss. Hedging involves precautionary buying or selling, contrary to the speculator's original expectations, if the market begins to behave differently from the manner anticipated. The currency speculator may be constantly adjusting his buying and selling and making new forward deals in order to avoid loss or to make certain of some profit.

Most speculation, especially in commodities, is fraught with danger since millions of pounds can be lost in a very short period. Financial institutions and banks need to keep a very strict control over their forward dealings. So do companies who buy commodities because they are forced to participate in the markets if they wish to remain in business.

Are There Any Controls in the Foreign Exchange Markets?

The United Kingdom abolished its exchange controls in 1979 as part of its efforts to reduce regulation and to expose the economy to free competition. Until then there had been a mixture of controls applied to the export and import of capital and the purchase of foreign exchange to finance deals. These controls stemmed from the war and the period of the post-war dollar shortage. Their intensity and extensiveness varied according to the nation's economic problems. At times, there were draconian restrictions on the amount that British tourists could take abroad. Most of the controls were aimed at outflows of capital. They inevitably generated a supervisory and regulatory bureaucracy and introduced an element of delay and uncertainty into commercial transactions. Most people were glad that they were abolished although there appeared to be a striking increase in the outflow of capital from the United Kingdom after they were ended. Some other countries have also abolished exchange controls on capital movements, for example, West Germany and the Netherlands. Belgium and Luxembourg have some controls still because they operate two exchange rates, one for current account payments and a second for capital payments. Italy has been reducing its controls and Denmark operates very few. Of the more advanced Community countries France had, until January 1990, the most extensive controls on capital which limited the ability of its citizens to hold bank accounts abroad. They also required permission to open foreign currency accounts in French banks, and there were restrictions on the ability of French banks to lend to non-residents. Some of these controls stemmed from the early period of socialist government under President Mitterrand when there was a flight of capital out of France. Inevitably, Greece, Spain and Portugal which have underdeveloped financial sectors have a higher degree of control over capital movements. None of the Community countries, however, approaches the Eastern bloc system of complete control of the inflow and outflow of currency. It is this control that enables the Soviet Union, for example, to impose a blatantly unrealistic exchange rate for the rouble on foreign visitors. Tourists quickly find that the 'free' market, or the 'black' market, exchange rate is many times more favourable, although taking advantage of it is illegal.

The Community intends to abolish controls on all capital movements from July 1990. Some countries will be allowed a partial reprieve until 1992, namely, Ireland, Spain, Portugal and Greece. They need not show complete compliance with the directive for that period. It is possible that Greece and Portugal may be given until 1995 to conform fully to the directive. There will be safeguards whereby a country can control short-term capital movements if there is a serious problem with its monetary or exchange rate policy.

It is intended that this relaxation of controls over capital movements will extend outside the Community to movements to and from non-Community countries. The long-term hope, therefore, is that trade, investments and financial markets will all benefit. Gradually, the freeing of capital movements will help to integrate the financial aspects of the Community. It will introduce more pressure to harmonise the rules and framework under which the banks and financial markets operate. If that harmony is achieved there will be even greater pressure for a common European currency and central bank.

Do Governments Allow Their Exchange Rates to Float Freely?

Very few governments leave their foreign exchange rates to the vagaries of the international markets. Some, like the USSR, go to the opposite extreme and try to control them completely, although there are indications that there is a change on the way. Others, like the United Kingdom, intervene in the markets when it suits their policy, but generally leave their currency to find its own level. Some, like most of the members of the European Community, get together and operate a coordinated or linked scheme to influence their rates. This scheme is called the European Monetary System (EMS).

Perhaps the most extensive and effective system of control of foreign exchange rates was that arising from the Bretton Woods agreement of 1944. This survived until 1971, although it suffered many vicissitudes. The agreement required countries to fix their exchange rates at a certain level which was notified to the International Monetary Fund (IMF). This rate was set at a level in relation to the price of gold but was, in effect, set against the dollar because the United States fixed the world price of gold in intergovernmental exchange. The country then needed to use its reserves to intervene in the foreign exchange markets to keep the rate within a band of 1 per cent above or below the central (par) rate. For example, the United Kingdom between 1949 and 1967 kept the pound between $2.82 and $2.78 with a central value of £1 = $2.80. For much of the time the rate was closer to the 'floor' price of $2.78 than to the 'par value'. In 1931, in the middle of the great international financial crisis the United Kingdom had left the old gold standard. It set up the Exchange Equalisation Account which contained the country's gold and other currency reserves. This fund of reserves was used to enter the foreign exchange markets to buy and sell currencies, including sterling, in order to keep the rate against the dollar at the required level. The markets were usually aware of the intervention but not of its extent. This system is essentially the same as the operation of 'buffer stock' buying and selling as in some world commodity agreements or in the Common Agricultural Policy.

Under the Bretton Woods agreement all the signatories used equivalents of the Exchange Equalisation Account to intervene in markets to influence their own rates of exchange. If they got into difficulties in this respect, or into balance of payments problems, they could ask the IMF for short-term loans to give them time to correct the situation and restore equilibrium. In the last resort, they could devalue their currency. The United Kingdom, for example, devalued the pound overnight from £1 = $2.80 to £1 = $2.40, in November 1967. The loans from the IMF were, and are, given provided that the country concerned took action to remove or reduce the fundamental causes of the problem. These might be high internal inflation, excessive government expenditure, or high costs of production reducing export competitiveness. The methods needed to tackle these problems – tax increases and cuts in government spending – were politically unpopular. The terms imposed by the IMF on the 1974–9 Labour government when it asked for loans were an important contributory factor to the unpopularity that led to its defeat in the 1979 election.

The Bretton Woods system of fixed parities which had to be defended, gradually broke down. Some countries such as Canada floated their currency. Others, like the United Kingdom, were very slow to devalue until forced. Stronger economies, like the West German were very slow to revalue, that is to raise the value of their currency. Governments increasingly felt that fixed foreign exchange rates imposed far too heavy a restraint on their internal economic policies. It was inevitable, therefore, that the growing international financial problems of the late 1960s and early 1970s should induce countries into trying a new panacea, freely floating foreign exchange rates accompanied by some intervention buying and selling.

This complete freedom was not, however, entirely suitable for the members of the European Community. They adopted temporary expedients of common exchange rate controls in the early 1970s. These were various versions of what became known as the 'snake in the tunnel'. This was a framework under which each country would have an upper and lower target limit for its exchange rate. Within this 'tunnel' the exchange rate could fluctuate. As the rate came near the outer limits the country needed to take corrective action. The rates of each participating country were interlinked or weighted in calculating the rates against the dollar. The system was modified over time but was not completely satisfactory because some countries were too slow, or ineffective, in taking remedial measures to correct problems. They were slow because the necessary measures were bound to be politically unpopular, since they usually included restraints on public and private expenditure. West Germany was sometimes slow to react despite the persistent strength of its economy and balance of payments. This was because it would have had to revalue the deutschmark upwards which would have cut the competitiveness of its exports. It was therefore necessary to develop another, more effective system.

Floating Exchange Rates and Monetarism

The politicians of the major economies succumbed to the siren songs of the economists who recommended floating exchange rates. They had reached their wits' end on measures to control inflation, rising unemployment, growing balance of payments deficits and budget deficits. When they were told that they could, in effect, have their cake and eat it, they seized on floating rates as the panacea for all their ills. They thought that they would free themselves from the shackles of having to make unpalatable and unpopular decisions about their internal economies in order to restore a balance of payments equilibrium or to maintain a narrow range of exchange rates. At the same time, the new priesthood of the resurrected theory of monetarism joined in the chorus.

This is not the place for a detailed explanation of what is called monetarism, a term that has come to have several meanings with the passage of time. In this context, however, we do need to know that the monetarists saw a direct relationship between changes in the quantity of money in circulation and the rate of change of the price level (inflation). Keynesian economists saw an indirect link because they allowed for excess demand and supply of money to be absorbed in a sort of 'buffer' in the shape of purchases and sales of bonds. The problem confronting the monetarists in practice was deciding what to count as 'money' and then how to control it. The financial world is such that as soon as you try to control something, the participants in the markets switch their assets or holdings into another type. Money takes many forms apart from the cash and notes with which we are all familiar. It includes all sorts of bills and bonds, bank deposits and liquid financial assets such as building society deposits, some of which are held in sterling and some in foreign currencies. One of the major problems of the pre-1979 period was that the British government had a very large borrowing requirement which was financed by the issue of long-term stock and by the sale of short-term bills (Treasury Bills). The methods they adopted were, according to the monetarists, the equivalent, to some extent, of 'printing money'. Thus any attempt to control the growth of the money supply involved the curtailing of government borrowing and, inevitably, cutbacks in public expenditure. This was successfully achieved by 1988 and the Treasury, with the help of the sale of public assets from the nationalised industries, enjoyed a large surplus of revenue over expenditure and was able to reduce the National Debt. This process was also supposed to have left extra funds available for the private sector to borrow for investment, that is, it ended what was called 'crowding out'. This was the name given to the process whereby the government, which was always able to pay as high an interest rate as was needed to get loans, could outbid the private sector.

One major aspect of the money supply problem was the movement into, and out of, the country of foreign funds. This movement is heavily influenced by the rate of interest prevailing in the United Kingdom compared with that in other comparable countries. High rates, other things being equal, attract larger deposits, and vice versa. The other influence is the level of the foreign exchange rate and expectations about its movements relative to other currencies in the future. Higher rates attract more foreign money into the country and tend to raise the foreign exchange rate. This cuts the effective price of imports and is deflationary, and tends to cut the demand for exports. This has a detrimental effect on the balance of payments (depending on the relative elasticities of supply and demand of imports and exports) and can contribute to large current account deficits.

Worse still was the significance of exchange rate intervention. Positive official financing involved buying pounds and selling foreign currency from the reserves in order to cut the exchange rate. An inevitable result was for domestic money supply also to be reduced, or to be increased by negative financing. Thus exchange rate policy constrained monetary policy in what, to monetarists, was an unacceptable way.

The United Kingdom adopted policies in the 1980s that were said to be monetarist, although many monetarists thought they were half hearted and insufficient. The main remaining weapon left to the Chancellor by 1988 was the ability to influence the interest rate. This was aimed at affecting the demand for money. Almost all the other controls over bank lending and asset ratios were abandoned. This was in contrast to West Germany which had an extensive and powerful set of controls over its banking sector. It could, as a result, control the supply of money as well. Consequently, Germany was able to have a low rate of inflation, a low level of interest rates and a heavy inflow of foreign capital.

The monetarists offered what appeared to be a simple explanation of inflation and an apparently straightforward set of solutions. All the government had to do was to control their money supply and to reduce their government spending and borrowing and everything would be all right. At the same time, they should try to improve the underlying efficiency of the economy by reducing costs on enterprise. These 'supply-side' improvements would reinvigorate a flagging national economy and generate a climate in which enterprise would flourish. Governments would be absolved from responsibility for balance of payments equilibrium and exchange rate levels. The system would be self-levelling and self-adjusting and no more politically unpopular measures resulting from balance of payments problems would be necessary.

These ideas were not equally well received in all European countries. Some were tried and rejected or modified. On the whole, the economic policies of Europe remained neo-Keynesian with some modifications. It can be argued, of course, that neo-Keynesian policies did not fail in the 1960s and 1970s but that the political will and nerve of politicians collapsed when it came to taking the remedial action required. They did too little, too late. The United States, which remained the power house of the international economy, was embroiled in the Vietnam War. Its mounting expenditure and deficits at home and abroad fuelled international inflation and disrupted money markets. Another problem was the mounting volume of oil revenues seeking investment outlets. Third World debt was also increasing rapidly. The growing oil revenues resulting from the price rises of the early 1970s shifted about the world looking for high returns and security. Their existence and movement affected exchange rates and interest rates. In the circumstances, it is no surprise that freely floating exchange rates were not fully adopted since most nations intervene to influence their foreign exchange rate. This is often called 'dirty floating' and its effectiveness depends to some extent on the size of the reserves with which the country can intervene. The Community adopted its own system arising from the need to make payments between members and to achieve some stability of its currencies in relation to each other. The European Monetary System was born.

What Is the European Monetary System?

The EMS comprises a European Monetary Cooperation Fund

(EMCF), an Exchange Rate Mechanism (ERM) and a currency, or unit of account, called an ECU. This stands for European Currency Unit in English but it was also a medieval French gold coin. The EMS was established in its present form in 1979. The United Kingdom has not yet joined the ERM (December, 1989) but participates in the other two elements. The Spanish peseta and Portuguese escudo were included for the first time in the calculation of the value of the ECU when its base was recalculated in September 1989. It can be seen that the frequently posed question 'should the United Kingdom join the EMS?' is badly phrased and is better put as 'should the United Kingdom join the Exchange Rate Mechanism?'

The European Monetary Cooperation Fund

The EMCF was set up in 1973 and acts as a mixture between the IMF and a Community central bank. The participants in the EMS deposit 20 per cent of their gold reserves and 20 per cent of their dollar reserves with the EMCF. In return they are credited with ECUs, the quantity of which credited to each country will change as the price of gold and dollars alters on world markets. The gold portion of the deposit with the EMCF is valued using six monthly averages of London gold prices and the dollar portion is valued at the market rate two days before the date of valuation. Thus both the world price of gold and the price of the dollar affect the quantity of ECUs created. Once credited to a country these ECUs can then be used to settle payments between members. The system is a foundation, via the ECU, for both a currency and an international reserve unit. The details of the deposits and their valuation in terms of dollars are reviewed every two years. The technicalities of the scheme are highly complex but there is no doubting the effectiveness of the institution. The number of ECUs in existence increases yearly and had reached 45 billion in 1985. The EMCF is at a disadvantage in that it cannot control the creation of ECUs because that is determined by the gold price and rate of the dollar.

The EMCF also has the function of making the Exchange Rate Mechanism work in the sense of facilitating payments between members. The intervention mechanism which is designed to make the ERM work obliges countries' central banks to give each other unlimited, very short-term credit facilities to finance required interventions. These loans and debts are paid through the EMCF in ECUs and interest is also paid in ECUs. As the single market is developed to 1992 more and more restrictions on banking and on movements of money will be relaxed. Regulations will be harmonised. It is possible that the EMCF and the ECU will both play an increasingly important part in the trend towards a new central bank and a currency for the Community.

The European Currency Unit

The ECU was a new name for the European Unit of Account (EUA), introduced in 1975, and has taken over all the functions of the EUA. From 1950 there had been a unit of account introduced by the European Payments Union (EPU) which was very straightforward in that it was based on the weight of gold in one US dollar. It was converted into national currencies at the official central rates for a member's currency, as determined by the Bretton Woods agreement. When that agreement began to break down in the early 1970s a number of different units of account were adopted, based on a variety of measures, some relatively stable, some fluctuating. The EUA replaced all these and was based on a specific quantity of each of the members' currencies. This was a copy of the Special Drawing Rights (SDRs) introduced by the IMF in 1969. The value of the SDRs was based upon an agreed 'basket' of sixteen different currencies weighted according to their relative importance.

The ECU then is a 'basket' currency which is used in the Community's budget, in payments between members and between them and African, Caribbean, Asian and Pacific members of the Lomé Convention. It is also used in Common Agricultural Policy payments, in the European Coal and Steel Community and in the European Investment Bank, and may be held as a reserve currency at the EMCF by non-members of the Community. Apart from these official uses there is a rapidly growing private market for the ECU: loans in ECUs can be raised by companies; you can buy travellers' cheques in ECUs; payments can be made in ECUs, and they are quoted on foreign exchange markets. In 1988, the United Kingdom government began issuing Treasury Bills in ECUs to finance some of its short-term borrowing requirements. The ECU is a genuine currency in international payments. It is not available as notes or coin, except for collectors, but is a unit of account, a store of value and a medium of exchange, that is it performs the traditional functions of money. There is every possibility that it will soon be an extra currency available alongside national currencies and usable by everyone in the Community. If so it is likely to replace the weaker currencies quite quickly.

How the ECU 'basket' is made up

The basket is re-examined every five years and was reconstituted in September 1989 to include the escudo and the peseta. The Greek drachma was included in September 1984. Table 7.1 shows the composition of the basket from September 1989.

TABLE 7.1
Percentage of EC National Currencies Contained in One ECU

Deutschmark	30.10
UK pound	13.00
French franc	19.00
Italian lira	10.15
Dutch guilder	9.10
Belgian franc	7.60
Luxembourg franc	0.30
Danish krone	2.45
Irish punt	1.10
Greek drachma	0.80
Spanish peseta	5.30
Portuguese escudo	0.80

You can look up the value of the pound in ECUs in the foreign exchange section of a newspaper. In November 1989 £1 = 1.4 ECU. The currency amounts given above have to be reviewed at the request of a country if its currency changes more than 25 per cent in 'weight' against the other currencies since the previous five yearly review.

The ECU is bought and sold on the foreign exchanges just like any other currency and it also features in futures and options markets. Over 10 billion are dealt in every day on the exchanges and their use is growing and extending. One of their attractions is their relative stability in the markets which tends to reduce some of the risks of international trading and financial transfers.

In order to calculate the value of the ECU, the central bank in each member state works out a representative market rate for its currency against the dollar. These rates together can then be used to calculate the dollar equivalent of the basket of Community currencies. The ECU is thus valued at the sum of the dollar equivalents of the currencies in the basket.

The Exchange Rate Mechanism

The mechanism was designed to help create what was called, when it was introduced in March 1979, 'a zone of monetary stability'. The United Kingdom did not join the mechanism, neither has Greece, and Spain and Portugal's participation has also not been resolved. There has been a long drawn out debate on whether the United Kingdom should join.

In order to create stability in the relationships of the exchange rates of the members, it was decided to replace the early 1970s' versions of the 'snake in the tunnel' systems referred to above with a grid system. Each participant establishes a central rate for its currency which is expressed in ECUs. The rate set has to be approved by all the members and is not set solely at the individual country's discretion.

The next step is to use these ECU expressed rates to work out a grid of bilateral exchange rates, for example between the deutschmark and the French franc. Once these bilateral rates are established a restriction is put upon the extent to which the market rates may diverge from the bilateral rates – usually up to 2.25 per cent on either side. These margins on either side of the bilateral rate are accompanied by 'divergence indicators' (see below). The Italian lira which is a more volatile currency has a 6 per cent margin rather than 2.25. It is likely that Greece, Spain and Portugal will initially be given a similar 6 per cent margin on either side of their central rate when their currencies join the ERM. If the United Kingdom ever joins there will be considerable debate about the desirable level of divergence to be granted and the length of the transition period. The crucial question, however, will be the level of the bilateral rate against the German mark.

Since 1979 there have been periods in which one or more countries' currencies have got into difficulties, leading to eleven realignments of the central rates between 1979 and 1989. These have usually involved revaluing the deutschmark and guilder and devaluing the lira and Belgian and French francs. Such readjustments must be done by agreement because every country's ECU related central rate is dependent on the rates of the other countries. The sequence of events, therefore, is for the bilateral rates to be renegotiated first after which the central rate is recalculated.

The divergence indicators

Divergence indicators are intended, first, to act as an early warning that a particular currency is deviating too much from the average, and, secondly, to provoke an early response before the gap grows too large. It is presumed in the EMS that a country will take appropriate action to restore the level of its currency and to remove or restrain the cause of its divergence. The system should encourage economic discipline and make governments work harder at controlling their inflation rates and public sector spending. They have not been completely successful in this because of the political reluctance of some governments to take the necessary measures. This is one reason why there have been eleven realignments in ten years.

What happens if a divergence indicator is reached?

If a currency touches its 2.25 margin above or below its bilateral rate against another country, it must take specific actions in its economic policies to readjust the relationship over time. The divergence indicator is set at a level to give it early warning to take action. In the short run it will indulge in intervention buying and selling, and is helped by the other country involved. In addition, the central bank with the strong currency buys the weak currency, and the central bank with the weak currency sells the strong currency. It may borrow from the 'strong' central bank if it does not have enough reserves to sell. These manipulations are conducted with the help of the EMCF and all the dealings are in ECUs. Any interest on loans is also paid in ECUs. The use of ECUs has the effect of sharing between the two countries the risk of any loss on the foreign exchange dealings.

What Has Been the Effect of the Exchange Rate Mechanism Since 1979?

The participants have very diverse economies with varying degrees of reliance upon foreign trade, and their balance of payments positions and rates of inflation differ greatly. West Germany has dominated the ERM because of its low inflation, steady growth and very healthy balance of payments surpluses. Italy has tended to be a problem, despite its greater 6 per cent range of latitude. The French economy has gone through bad patches but has recovered. In the face of this variety the ERM has, on the whole, achieved a remarkable degree of stability of exchange rates for its participants in a period when world exchange rates have been volatile. The study of comparative exchange rate movements is beset with statistical problems, but the rates of the currencies within the grid seem to have been less subject to the extremes of fluctuation than those outside it. This is not necessarily entirely due to them being in the ERM but the supporters of the EMS believe that it is.

Why Did the United Kingdom Not Join the ERM?

The Labour government of 1974 to 1979 was a weak government reliant on the support of minority parties. Despite the referendum which strongly supported the United Kingdom's continued membership, there was a powerful element in the party and Cabinet which regarded the Community as an alien authority. They feared deeper involvement in any enterprise which appeared to them to be non-socialist in aspiration or from which they could not easily escape. The government faced severe difficulties in its economic management. The inflation rate and level of unemployment were rising rapidly. A succession of incomes policies was tried and found wanting, culminating in the breakdown of the 'social contract' and the subsequent 'winter of discontent'. The balance of payments and the value of the pound were both subject to unusual pressures because of the inflow of capital to exploit North Sea oil development. Large loans had been raised from the IMF and other groups of international lenders. It was thus not thought to be a good time to embark on what was seen as another uncertainty by joining the ERM. It may be that the government was not willing to accept the required levels of discipline to make the pound fit within the ERM, regarding it as a surrender of sovereignty over our economic policies.

Why Has the United Kingdom Not Joined the ERM Since 1979?

Between 1979 and 1989 the pound has fluctuated between wide extremes. As a result there has been a sharp conflict between those whose interest is in having a low exchange rate, mainly against the dollar (that is exporters), and those who favour a high rate (that is importers). For a time, the pound, on a tide of oil, reached the 1967 devaluation rate of £1 = $2.40. This had a devastating effect on manufacturing industry and was partially responsible, together with high interest rates, for the destruction of the United Kingdom's manufacturing base in the early 1980s. Then, for a while, the pound fell so low that experts were predicting a £1 = $1 exchange rate. There are, however, reasons for this greater volatility of the pound. Sterling is more important than the other European currencies in international trade and finance. The general point of importance, though, is that there is no real agreement on what is a reasonable, workable rate of exchange against the dollar, the deutschmark and the yen. The government has had no genuinely consistent policy with relation to the exchange rate except to let it float in accordance with market forces. It has, periodically, intervened to halt a movement or to nudge it in a certain direction and its interest rate policies have sometimes had an exchange rate dimension, that is influencing the flow of capital into and out of sterling.

Although there was a lack of a coherent, interventionist policy, a consensus of opinion grew up that strongly favoured the United Kingdom's entry into the ERM. Thus, by 1987, it appeared that Mrs Thatcher, with a few loyal supporters, was the only obstacle to joining, and there was a major difference of opinion between her and the Treasury and the Bank of England. This position has gradually changed since mid 1988 as more economists have analysed the hypothetical effects of the United Kingdom's joining. They have become more cautious in their support and some have become critical of the possible effects. One cause of the change was the revelation that Mr Lawson, the Chancellor of the Exchequer, had been following a policy of keeping sterling in step with the German mark for about a year, with a view to joining the ERM. A number of economic events undermined this policy and Mrs Thatcher disapproved of the degree of intervention required in the foreign exchange markets.

In the final analysis, however, the main reason why the United Kingdom has not joined the Exchange Rate Mechanism is the fear of loss of economic sovereignty and the reluctance to accept externally imposed discipline over economic policy. There is a lack of agreement about what level to set for the pound against the mark and there are problems about the percentage allowed initially for divergence from the central rate. These could be resolved. The real difficulty is a psychological one related to national pride, independence and sovereignty.

Will the Single Market in 1992 Have Much Impact on Money and Banking?

There will be enormous changes as the directives implementing the single market are implemented. It is the intention that the movement of services and capital should be freed from artificial restrictions as well as goods and people. This will involve the dismantling, in most states, of a range of restrictions on the holding and transfer of capital and currency. The United Kingdom has relatively few controls except those required to prevent fraud and to protect the customer, the shareholder and the depositor. It is partly this lack of controls that has enabled the City of London to retain its pre-eminence in European financial markets. However, there is a long-term threat to this position as the European markets are freed. The French stock exchange and other financial markets are being modernised. German banks are becoming more international. There is a real risk that the City will fail to put enough resources into European financial centres to exploit the new markets. There is also a threat to the City in that the new Community rules may, in some respects, make London less attractive to non-European banks such as the Japanese, Arabian and American. There will also be significant changes in the framework within which insurance services will operate. These will, theoretically, provide great opportunities in Europe for British companies which already have a major international role. A general fear of some British commentators is that the single market will impose a more bureaucratic regulatory framework than exists in the United Kingdom today. This, it is argued, partly defeats the objective of freeing the Community from restrictions.

These rather mundane areas of advance have been overshadowed by the row that developed in 1988 between Mrs Thatcher and other members of the Community, notably Jacques Delors, the President of the Commission. This concerns the idea that the single market and the freeing of capital movements makes inevitable the creation of a Community central bank and a single Community currency. Mrs Thatcher has dismissed this idea as nonsense despite public opinion polls that indicate that the British people would not mind a European currency. M. Delors is, of course, right. A single market for capital, a European Monetary System based on the ECU and an Exchange Rate Mechanism all indicate the need for a single, or super, European central bank and a single currency based on the ECU. Mrs Thatcher may delay their introduction but they will arrive in due course. We would all benefit from a single currency. A Euro MP once explained to the European Parliament that if you started with £100 in cash and changed it into francs and then into lira and so on until you had successively bought all the currencies of the Community, and then bought back pounds, you would only have £26 left. Thus £74 would have gone on commission without your having bought anything! The logic of a single currency will eventually get through. Indeed, there has already been considerable growth in the use of the ECU by private business and some individuals. There is a danger that the other major countries of the Community will go ahead in this respect without the United Kingdom and the pound.

The creation of a central bank for the Community might pose more problems, especially for economic nationalists, but again the EMCF is already a powerful influence and could be adapted to the role. The United Kingdom is again very concerned about economic sovereignty. The impartial observer might say that the European performance, especially that of the West German Bundesbank, is superior to that of the Bank of England in recent years. Thus the United Kingdom would do well to pool what little of the sovereignty remains to the Bank of England and Treasury with the Europeans. Many economists say that this sovereignty is, in any case, very severely constrained. It is impossible for the United Kingdom to operate an independent policy in the face of the other economic forces in the world, such as the deutschmark, the dollar and the yen. Britain is, moreover, reduced to having only one shot left in its locker – interest rate changes. The City, if not Mrs Thatcher, appears to be recognising that its future self-interest lies in a European commitment, including a single currency and European central bank. These might initially be alongside existing central banks and currencies.

Perhaps the most telling statement was made by Sir Leon Brittan, British Commissioner and Vice President of the Commission, who said, in February 1989, that 'the EMS has succeeded in providing the structure within which movement between member currencies has been significantly limited. The role of the deutschmark as linchpin of the system has led to a convergence on a low inflation level for those countries in the ERM: this has been a highly constructive development both for them and for the cohesion of the Community generally.' He went on to argue that it would be advantageous for the United Kingdom to join the ERM for three reasons: first, because joining the ERM now would be a clear signal to the financial markets that the United Kingdom's political commitment to low inflation had been given institutional form; secondly, the United Kingdom's full membership of the EMS would put it in a far more favourable position from which to help guide its future development; lastly, membership of the EMS would be of benefit to British business and industry by providing for the first time a framework within which receipts from goods exported to the Community could be planned in sterling terms.

It is probable that practical views such as this will eventually prevail over the more emotional, national sovereignty attitudes of Mrs Thatcher and her close supporters, and the United Kingdom will embrace the Exchange Rate Mechanism and become a full member of the European Monetary System. If they do not prevail then Frankfurt may replace the City of London as the main financial centre of Europe.

The Social Integration of Europe

Introduction

The nations of Europe are likely to retain their distinctive characters for many centuries to come, but the very existence of the Community will tend to create greater uniformity of approach in vital areas of daily life. This will happen largely because of institutional and legal pressures to conform, but there will also be a considerable informal pressure arising from the natural human characteristic of copying successful methods and procedures. The process has already gone a long way in the original Six members despite the differentiating marks of language and history. It is continuing with the second group of members, including the United Kingdom. In this context three areas in particular are worth looking at in greater depth: law and justice, social policy itself, and environmental policy.

Law and Justice

It is the application of law which distinguishes civilisation from anarchy. Thus a study of the European Community should probably start from a detailed examination of its legal base. The Community is unique – there has never been a national or international system like it – and is based on a new, autonomous and uniform body of law that is separate from national law. This body of law also transcends national law and is applied directly in all member states.

In order to make sure that there was a uniform interpretation and application of this law the Community set up the Court of Justice, based in Luxembourg. Its job is to ensure that the law is observed when the treaties establishing the Community are applied and interpreted.

The origins of Community law

The major source of Community law lies in the 'primary' legislation created by the members. This consists of the Treaties of Paris and Rome in particular, plus various Conventions and the Treaties of Accession when new members join. It also includes association agreements with non-members such as Turkey (1963) and the First Lomé Convention of 1975 with African, Caribbean and Pacific countries. These treaties and agreements have had numerous additions made to them as time has passed. These additions are called protocols, schedules or annexes and count as 'primary' legislation.

The other important written source is called 'secondary' legislation and is the law created by the Community institutions. It usually takes the form of directives, regulations and 'decisions' which may be addressed to states or to individuals.

There are also some international agreements reached by the Community as a whole. The most important of these relate to tariffs and trade. These agreements are implemented by directives and decisions and thus become Community law rather than remaining as international law.

Community law has, in addition, an unwritten basis. Various articles of the Treaties of Rome say that the Court of Justice must look at the general principles of law as well as at the written law. The treaties say nothing about fundamental rights so it is essential to apply general principles in this area.

There is also what is called 'customary law' which results from established practice. The best example is the right of the European Parliament to question the Council of Ministers. This derives from custom.

The Court of Justice frequently applies the general rules of international law. These are regarded only as a supplementary source of Community law because they tend to be very generalised.

An important source of law in the Community stems from

decisions made by the Council of Ministers. The ministers represent their governments so technically these 'decisions' are governmental agreements and, therefore, international conventions. These decisions are taken by the ability of each state to act under international law, not under power conferred by the Community treaties. There is still some debate as to whether these decisions, based as they are on international conventions, are technically Community law, but they are in practice which is what matters.

The Court of Justice

Since 1986 the court has consisted of thirteen judges assisted by six advocates-general. They each have two assistants, legal clerks who do research for them on the case and on procedure, and who prepare documents for them. The judges and advocates-general have their independence guaranteed by law. They are irremovable; they deliberate in secret and are immune from legal proceedings against them unless the court itself waives the immunity.

The appointment of members of the court is done by agreement by member governments. The judges sit for six years and may have their term of office renewed. Membership is arranged so that every three years there is a partial replacement of judges. There is no nationality requirement but there is one judge from each state, the thirteenth judge always coming from one of the larger states. The judges have a variety of backgrounds apart from recently practising law or being a judge. Some of them have been diplomats, some politicians, some academics and some senior officials. They must be chosen from 'persons whose independence is beyond doubt and who possess the qualifications required for appointment to the highest judicial offices in their respective countries or who are proconsuls of recognised competence'.

The judges choose a president from among themselves. He acts for three years directing the court, allocating cases, appointing a judge as rapporteur for each case and determining the schedules for hearings. He may act alone to give judgment in summary proceedings on applications for provisional measures but his decision may be referred to the full court.

The advocates-general are appointed on the same terms as the judges. They are assigned to cases and their job is 'to act with complete impartiality and independence and to make, in open court, reasoned submissions on cases brought before the Court in performance of the tasks assigned to it'.

The court conducts most of its business in plenary session, with a quorum of seven judges. Cases brought by member states or institutions of the Community must be heard in plenary session. The court may, however, operate in 'chambers'. There are four chambers composed of three judges, and two chambers composed of six judges. The chambers take cases in rotation and do not specialise. Cases brought by individuals or firms may be referred to chambers rather than to the full court.

The Single European Act of February 1986 will lead to the attachment of a 'Court of First Instance' to the Court of Justice. This will hear cases brought by officials of the Community, competition cases and actions for damages. It will not hear actions brought by member states nor deal with questions referred for preliminary rulings. There will be an appeal from its decisions to the Court of Justice on points of law.

It is important to realise that, although the Court of Justice is the Community's supreme judicial body and that there is no appeal against its judgments, other national courts at all levels also apply Community laws.

The role of the Court of Justice

In the beginning the court dealt mainly with the problems arising from establishing a customs union. This led, gradually, to common rules on transport, agriculture and an assortment of freedoms such as the right to establish a business anywhere, the right to provide services, and freedom of competition. Increasingly, the work of the court moved into social areas and to the consideration of the freedom of workers, the right to social security and the rights of migrant workers. As with any legal system a number of important cases are quoted as test cases. They have established certain principles which have been accepted as precedents. The American Supreme Court did the same in the first few decades of its existence. In both Europe and America there is a slow evolution over time as cases are brought before the courts.

In principle a court can order an individual, firm or institution to do something it is supposed to do, to stop doing something it should not do, and to do something differently. It can also draw up limitations on the scope of their actions. These various forms of action have precise names:

(a) *Proceedings for failure to fulfil an obligation* There have been over 400 cases under this heading since 1953. Some have been brought by member state against other members because of alleged failure to meet regulations, for example on the free movement of sheep meat or restrictions on fishing. Usually, the states comply with the court's ruling by modifying their national laws. Occasionally, they stall until another action is brought. If the member is desperately keen to continue its policy it may use delaying tactics until the Community rules are changed.

(b) *Proceedings for annulment* These are a way of reviewing the legality of Commission decisions and regulations and of settling conflicts over the respective powers of the various institutions of the Community. There have been very few actions brought by member states against the Council of Ministers. There have, however, been about forty actions brought by them against Commission decisions. These have related to whether national financial help is lawful, to transport, to the free movement of goods and to the settlement of agricultural payments. A few cases have been brought against the European Parliament. It, for its part, once intended to take the Council to the court over a budget dispute but withdrew when the Council gave way. The court has, subsequently, in 1985, had to settle a dispute between the Council and the Parliament.

(c) *Failure to act* These proceedings in the court enable people to punish inactivity which can be damaging. Most of these proceedings have been declared inadmissible, especially those from private individuals and firms. They can only be admissible if the institution in question has previously been called upon to act. In the early 1970s, in a celebrated case, the Parliament brought such an action against the Council of Ministers for failure to act to introduce elections to the Parliament by direct election and universal suffrage, instead of indirect appointment. The court's decision was pre-empted by the 1974 agreement of the Heads of Governments to hold direct elections.

(d) *Actions to establish liability* The court has the exclusive

jurisdiction to order that the Community pays damages because of its actions or its legislative acts. This is on the principle of non-contractual liability. The Community's contractual liability is dealt with by the individual members' laws and courts.

The Court of Justice acts in the above ways. Thus member states may be brought to observe the law and a greater uniformity of practice is assured. The general long-term effect of the court has been to speed up social and commercial integration.

How do Community law and national law mix?

We tend to hear most about conflicts between Community law and national law because the question of sovereignty is involved. There is, however, a great area of positive interplay between them where no obvious conflict arises.

The area of interplay is where Community law refers to the members' legal systems in order to complete its own requirements. For example, freedom of movement and the right to establish businesses is given only to nationals of the members. It is left to the member states to decide with their own laws who is a national of their state.

Sometimes Community law uses the national law's legal institutions to add to its own rules. This is usual with the enforcement of judgments of the Court of Justice. An article of the Treaty of Rome says that enforcement is to be governed by the rules of civil procedure in the state concerned. In addition, the treaty sometimes refers to the general principles common to the laws of the members.

Despite the wide areas of agreement or interplay referred to, there are conflicts between Community law and member states' laws because the Community law sometimes creates direct rights and obligations for its citizens. These apply directly to member states and may not be consistent with the rule of the national law. In such instances, one of the systems has to give way. There is no written Community law that resolves this problem. Nowhere does it say that Community law takes precedence over national law. Yet it is obvious that it must if the Community is to survive.

The issue of conflict is, in practice, resolved by the Community law having precedence, the basis of which is aimed at ensuring *the ability of the Community to function*. The members have given the

Community the legislative powers to function and it would not be able to do so if its legislation were not binding on all its members. The Community could not continue if members could annul its laws at any time that it suited their national convenience to do so. The legal consequence of this is that any provision of national law which conflicts with Community law is invalid.

These conclusions have been established over the years by a series of cases before the Court of Justice. The most important of these was the 1961 case of *Costa* v. *ENEI*. At the end of the summing up the court said 'it follows from all these observations that the law stemming from the Treaty, an independent source of law, could not, because of its special and original nature, be overridden by domestic legal provisions, however framed, without being deprived of its character as Community law and without the legal basis of the Community itself being called into question'.

Later cases related to national constitutional law. The Dutch have removed any potential problem by writing the precedence of Community law into their constitution. Germany and Italy have constitutional courts which make an exception to the principle of the supremacy of Community law where it conflicts with their constitutional guarantees. They argue that any dispute should be settled in favour of fundamental rights.

The United Kingdom has no separate written constitution and no explicit Bill of Rights, although it does subscribe to the European Convention on Human Rights. It is assumed that United Kingdom citizens have rights unless they are explicitly removed by law. It is clear that many British parliamentarians and commentators have been very surprised at the extent to which Community law is impinging on British law and new legislation. As the Single European Act is implemented it is clear that their views of national sovereignty need to be revised to take account of the supremacy of Community law.

The Social Policy of the European Community

The social policies of the European Community originated in the European Coal and Steel Community (ECSC). This intended to rationalise the two industries so it was inevitable that the social implications should be considered. Thus one of the ECSC's objectives was 'to promote improved living and working conditions for the workers'. This involved provisions for redeployment, safety, retraining, resettlement, guaranteed adequate wages, free movement of workers and safeguarded entitlement to social security benefits.

The European Community took over these objectives although they were not always expressed in exactly the same form. There were also important additions, notably the adoption of the principle of equal pay for equal work for men and women and an emphasis on harmonisation of standards among member states. The Community also set up a Social Fund whose objective was to promote employment opportunities and geographical and occupational mobility for workers within the Community. An area of particular interest was social security for migrant workers. Minimum health and safety standards were also established by the Euratom Treaty.

The European Social Fund

The ESF was set up by the Treaty of Rome in Articles 123 to 127. The fund has been reformed on several occasions since, in 1971, in 1977 and 1983. In 1988, a major review began and it is intended to implement changes by 1990.

The fund obtains its money from the Community budget. In 1988, the ESF budget was £2,122 million. In 1987, the United Kingdom received £405 million from the Social Fund. Usually, the money is allocated to match that put up by public bodies in the country concerned. The Social Fund, and for that matter the Regional Fund, has to compete with the Common Agricultural Policy (CAP) for money. The CAP has its own fund for 'guidance and restructuring', the European Agricultural Guidance and Guarantee Fund (EAGGF in English or FEOGA in French). This has helped to finance the less favoured areas of farming and has provided money for small farmers who wish to leave the industry. In the 1970s and the early 1980s the demands of the CAP expanded rapidly, especially on the price guarantee side, and prevented any significant growth in the Social or Regional Funds.

The European Parliament and Community politicians found this increasingly frustrating. This frustration partly explains the willingness to curtail agricultural spending. There was a slow growth in expenditure by both funds but this did not match the problems that arose from widespread unemployment and industrial decline after

1973. The difference in emphasis on the programmes can be seen from the 1985 budget which appropriated about 67 per cent of the total for agricultural guarantees and another $2\frac{1}{2}$ per cent for agricultural guidance and other specific measures. In contrast, the appropriation for the Regional Fund was 7.5 per cent of the total budget and 6.5 per cent for the Social Fund. The other areas which received relatively little support in many people's view were assistance to developing countries and food aid. This amounted to about 3 per cent of the total budget although this represented a large increase of about 30 per cent over the previous year's allocation. The hope is, therefore, that now the agricultural spending seems to be under control, more money can be devoted to the Social Fund, the Regional Fund and overseas aid.

On the financial side of the social policy, one of the recent problems has been created by the accession of Greece, Spain and Portugal. These have, in varying degrees, higher unemployment, lower incomes per head and lower standards of social provision. The same conditions apply in some areas of Italy. The Community has responded by raising the budget for expenditure from the Regional and Agricultural Guidance Funds from £5 billion in 1985 to £9 billion by 1992. Between 60 and 70 per cent of the total funds will be spent in Portugal, Greece and parts of Spain and Italy. Ireland is also included in this group. In 1985, there were also established some special schemes called Integrated Mediterranean Programmes. These will be used to develop the Mediterranean areas of France, Italy and Greece. They are aimed at reducing high unemployment and economic weakness, and raising living standards. They will provide training facilities, protect the environment and improve agriculture, fishing and the infrastructure. There is another programme to help Portugal. This is called PEDIP which is intended to improve Portuguese productivity and the quality of its goods.

One of the strengths of the Community is the way in which it can muster resources and target them at disadvantaged areas. The assumption is, of course, that market forces will not, in themselves, rectify the economic backwardness of the regions mentioned.

What areas does social policy cover?

The following list will give some idea of the pervasiveness of the policy. These items cannot be discussed individually in any depth and the reader is recommended to obtain, free, a copy of 'The Social Policy of the European Community' from the Office for Official Publications of the European Communities, if detail is required. It will be obvious, however, that simply listing the items reveals a great possibility of conflict between the United Kingdom government and the Community. The prevailing pro-market, anti-interventionist policy in the United Kingdom is very different from the social democratic, interventionist tone of the Community's social policy.

The areas covered by the policy include:

Free movement of workers
Social security for migrant workers
Promotion of workers' geographical and occupational mobility
Equal pay for men and women
Safety at work
Health protection in the nuclear industry
Working hours and holidays
Vocational retraining
Handicapped persons, elderly workers
Youth unemployment
Full and better employment-coordinating national policies
Redeployment of workers in declining industries
Leisure of workers, housing
Accident prevention and health protection
Integration of migrant workers
Help for the neediest – homeless, old, vagrants, one-parent families
Industrial democracy, workers' participation
Rights of working women

The penultimate item in the list, industrial democracy and workers' participation, is beginning to create problems for the United Kingdom government. Having 'defeated' the unions between 1979 and 1986, it now faces the unwelcome prospect of the Community putting trade unionists on the board of management of all companies above a certain size. The fact that most European countries see this as right, sensible and constructive seems to escape the British government.

From the lengthy list given above it may be useful to examine one area in detail, the rights of working women.

How has social policy affected the rights of working women?

Article 119 of the Treaty of Rome said that pay differentials between men and women should be abolished by the end of 1961. This deadline was not achieved and it was reset at the end of 1964. This delay was despite the fact that most of the written constitutions of the members include guarantees of the equality of the sexes. It became apparent as time passed that women remained in a relatively unprivileged position both in the labour market and socially. In 1975, therefore, the Council of Ministers adopted a directive which required member states to repeal all laws, regulations and administrative provisions that were not compatible with the principle of equal pay. They were also ordered to ensure that the principle was integrated into collective agreements and individual contracts. They were to enable any woman to claim her rights before the courts without fear of dismissal. A year later, in 1976, a supplement to this directive gave members two and a half years to give equal treatment to men and women in access to employment, vocational training, promotion and working conditions. They had to abolish all legal provisions and any terms of collective agreements that were prejudicial to working women. These directives have led to extensive changes to British law.

There still remained, however, areas of discrimination, for example in the application of social security. At the end of 1987 member states were given a six-year period in which to introduce equality of treatment. This includes the abolition of discrimination in respect of sex, marital or family status, the coverage of social security schemes, the obligation to pay contributions and the calculation of benefits and allowances.

Since then the Commission has insisted on receiving regular reports from each country on its progress in implementing the directives. It has followed up any failures to do so by threatening reference to the Court of Justice and has, on several occasions, brought actions against recalcitrant member states. Private individuals have also brought cases before their national courts and later appealed to the European Court of Justice.

As an extension of its efforts the Commission organised an action programme between 1982 and 1985 on promoting equal opportunities for women. No one pretends that equality has yet been achieved especially when the evidence of inequality of earnings, and so on, is seen, but the Community has made effective progress towards creating a proper legislative framework for equality. This has probably gone much further than a United Kingdom government left to its own devices would have done.

Conclusion

The evidence is that the United Kingdom has been forced or dragged along by the Community at a pace faster than it would have adopted on its own. The United Kingdom is still near the bottom of the European league in terms of social security provision, hours of work, inspection of health and safety at work, and overall social welfare. The United Kingdom is also far behind in relation to worker participation in management and decision-making. It is probable that the changes required under the Single European Act and the harmonisation of the social market will work wonders for the British economy. The powers of the Council are limited in respect of social policy under the Act. Unanimity is required in the Council of Ministers. Decisions by majority are not allowed in the area of social policy but, once again, the other members might go ahead without Britain. If the United Kingdom did go ahead with the same general approach as the other members, it might pull the United Kingdom's social policies out of the Victorian age.

The Community and the Environment

The word 'environment' is usually used in a subjective as well as objective sense to refer to the quality of the air, the water, countryside, soil, sea and animal life around us. This quality is heavily influenced by the size of population and its density. This, together with income per head, determines the other major factor influencing the quality of the environment, that is energy use. These three forces, population size, population density and energy use tend to predetermine the nature and scale of environmental problems. These difficulties can, of course, be alleviated or aggravated by Community policy. Some people allege that the Common Agricultural Policy is responsible for considerable ecological damage with its stimulation of arable farming and the 'excessive' use of fertiliser and pesticides.

It should always be remembered when discussing environmental issues that they nearly always have an international aspect. The United Kingdom's power station gases may be Western Europe's acid rain. A chemical works putting effluent into the Rhine affects the quality of the North Sea. A Chernobyl disaster, or atmospheric test of a nuclear device, spreads a radioactive swathe across several continents. It is this international feature of environmental affairs that makes the European Community peculiarly valuable because it has the administrative machinery already in place to act quickly in pursuit of a coordinated policy.

What is the population background?

In 1986, the population density of the twelve members of the Community was 143 per square kilometre. This compares with 324 in Japan, 26 in the United States and 12 in the USSR. It is expected that all these figures will rise by the year 2000, the Community figure by about 2. The figures for European countries show a wide range, as is clear from Table 8.1.

Crude measures of overall density are only a start to analysing basic pressures. We also need to have data on urbanisation and population movements over time. It is urbanisation which produces the undesirable concentrations of atmospheric pollution from vehicles and industry, creating the need for extensive systems for the collection and disposal of refuse and sewage. The very act of creating urban areas destroys natural habitats, trees and hedgerows. It requires large volumes of raw materials such as timber and aggregates like sand and gravel. Urban growth is accompanied by extensive road building, power lines, pipelines, reservoirs, pumping stations, sewerage works and railways. This process involves the exploitation of natural resources, many of which are from the Third World. Since there is relatively little stress on the recycling of materials this represents a high level of new demand.

The growth of communications and the ownership of the private motor car now ensure that no area is free from exploitation. There has been a remarkable expansion of urbanisation, for example, in the areas of the Community blessed by sun and sea. High incomes and the trend to early retirement have accelerated this movement, nor are inland or mountain areas safe if they are suitable for leisure developments. As a result, seas and lakes are prone to many forms of

TABLE 8.1
Population Density

1986	Inhab. Km²	Total Area Km²	Agricultural Area in Use Approx. %
Belgium	323	30 500	45
Denmark	119	43 100	65
West Germany	246	248 700	47
Greece	75	132 000	40
Spain	77	504 000	53
France	101	549 100	57
Ireland	50	70 300	81
Italy	190	301 300	58
Luxembourg	143	2 600	49
Netherlands	349	41 785	49
Portugal	110	92 389	49
United Kingdom	232	244 100	74
Europe 12	143	2 260 680	58
World	37	135 837 000	

SOURCE   Eurostat, *Basic Statistics of the Community*, 25th edn (Luxembourg: Office for Official Publications of the European Communities, 1988).

pollution. Since water touches or crosses many frontiers and derives from rain or melting snow, even a nation which actively pursues a sound environmental policy may be at the mercy of its 'dirty' neighbours. The United Kingdom has had the unenviable reputation in the 1970s and 1980s of being the 'dirty man of Europe' because its atmospheric pollution drifts on the prevailing westerly winds over to Scandinavia and Western Europe. Excuses are uttered and the United States is also blamed but only gradually have effective counter-measures been taken. In the autumn of 1988, Mrs Thatcher donned a 'green' mantle in a major speech and there are signs that more action will be taken on atmospheric pollution from industry, on exhaust emissions, water quality and the disposal of waste into the sea.

Fortunately, the expected population growth of Europe is marginal. This provides an opportunity to implement effective policies that are built into all areas of agricultural, commercial and industrial expansion. It is perhaps as well to keep the issue in perspective. In the Community, in 1985, only 8.5 per cent of land was classified as 'built up'; 58.8 per cent was agricultural; 22.1 per cent 'wooded'; 1.6 per cent was 'inland water'; 9 per cent had 'other uses'. If enough money and political will is forthcoming then those elements which arise from within the Community can be controlled. Those elements arising outside the Community, such as the destruction of tropical rain forest, require international action. Again, it is fortunate that 'green' politics have become very important, especially in West Germany and Scandinavia. The political will seems to exist to make environmental considerations paramount, although in the Netherlands the government was brought down in May 1989 because it tried to push control of the private motor car too far.

How significant is energy use in the Community in the environmental context?

Of the Community countries only the United Kingdom and the Netherlands have an energy surplus. These surpluses arise from oil and natural gas. As a result the Community in 1985 imported 43 per cent of its primary energy requirements. In contrast, the United States imported only 12 per cent while Japan, at the other extreme, imported 82 per cent. The USSR produced a surplus of 21 per cent. The Community has worked very hard to reduce energy imports since the first oil crisis of 1973. Imports were then 60 per cent of consumption (see Table 8.2).

Oil accounts for about 45 per cent of European primary energy requirements. The transport and burning of oil is probably the major environmental hazard. Nuclear power is growing in importance especially in France where it is used to generate about 70 per cent of the electricity. Over the years since 1973 industry has managed to reduce its share of energy consumption from 35 to 29 per cent. In the household and services sector consumption has been a static share of the total. In the field of transport, however, there has been a rise from 18 to 25 per cent. This is largely accounted for by the growth of private car ownership, despite the greater fuel efficiency of modern vehicles.

TABLE 8.2
Production and Consumption of Primary Energy: Europe 12

	Production %	Consumption %
Oil	25.6	45.0
Coal and lignite	28.7	23.1
Natural gas	21.6	18.0
Nuclear energy	21.3	12.2
Hydroelectric	2.8	1.7
Total	589 million T.E.P.	1029 million T.E.P.

T.E.P. = tonnes of oil equivalent.
SOURCE Eurostat, *Europe in Figures* (Luxembourg: Office for the Official Publications of the European Communities, 1988).

Energy consumption has several main implications for the environment. The extraction of coal is usually environmentally harmful. The extraction and transport of oil is accompanied by potential risks as with the *Torrey Canyon*, *Amoco Cadiz* and *Piper Alpha* disasters. Nuclear energy for electricity generation carries the greatest long-term hazard to the environment, although enormous expenditures and engineering skills go into reducing this risk factor. The greatest immediate hazards, however, come from the burning of hydrocarbon fuels, coal, oil and natural gas. The emissions from this burning pollute their immediate environment and, through the atmosphere, the environment hundreds or thousands of miles away. In addition, the production, use and dispersal of chemicals and plastics sometimes has an accumulative deleterious effect on the environment.

Has the Community developed a coherent policy on the environment?

The answer to this question is a qualified 'yes'. There is still a debate about the detail and the timing of initiatives but a policy should be in place by 1992. Some countries appear to be more susceptible than others to pressure from industry to delay and procrastinate. The United Kingdom has lagged behind in terms of water purity standards, beach cleanliness, the control of vehicle exhaust emissions and the use of unleaded petrol. There is considerable argument about standards for food, food processing and animal husbandry. Another serious dispute concerns the treatment and disposal of toxic waste. Once again, the United Kingdom is called the 'dustbin' of Europe because it has placed stress upon private enterprise controlling disposal sites and the provision of incinerators for all sorts of dangerous chemical waste. To the intense anger of the environment lobby much of this waste is imported. Sellafield has now been expanded to become the major European nuclear waste processing plant.

It is hard for the lay person to find a way through the labyrinth of statistics and propaganda that emanates from governments and pressure groups. Environmental and ecological pressure groups have multiplied like rabbits over the last twenty years. They all want government, Community or international action of some sort. Frequently, this involves large expenditure or additional costs on producers or users. The scene is then set for a clash of pressure groups. Usually, the producers' lobby is financially stronger and more skilled at manipulating the political decision-making process. Eventually, the environmental lobby may triumph in whole or in part through the persuasion of public opinion, as in the suspension by most countries of whaling, or in the international agreement in May 1989 to suspend the use of CFCs by the year 2000. Gradually, governments may see votes in appeasing the 'green' lobby. Alternatively, reports from its research institutions may provoke them into belated action as in the banning of CFCs in plastics and aerosols in order to protect the ozone layer, as mentioned above. It is probably fair to say that the United Kingdom has rarely been at the forefront of environmental progress in the Community. Its role, despite recent protestations, has been a cautious, tending to the negative, one.

How has the Community policy developed?

In 1972, there was a major United Nations Conference on the Environment in Stockholm. The Community Heads of Government later in 1972 acknowledged that economic growth had to be linked to improvements in living standards and the quality of life of its citizens and to protection of the environment and natural resources. They concluded that 'economic expansion is not an end in itself'.

The Heads of Government laid out a thirteen-point programme and asked the Commission to formulate a Community environment policy. This was done and in late 1973 the Community's first programme began. It lasted four years and was followed by a second and third. The fourth programme began in 1987 and will operate until 1992. Up to 1987 over a hundred pieces of legislation had been enacted although not all the tight deadlines specified had been met. The programme adopted outlined three main spheres of action:

1. the reduction and prevention of pollution and nuisances;
2. the improvement of the environment and the quality of life;
3. action by the Community, or where applicable, by united action of the members, in international organisations concerned with the environment.

The Commission had tried to define 'the environment' as 'the combination of elements whose complex interrelationships make up the settings, the surroundings and the conditions of life of the individual and of society, as they are, or as they are felt'. This broad definition includes the man-made environment such as the architectural heritage as well as the natural world.

The Heads of Government had agreed on some very important principles that have been included in subsequent statements. For example, the Single European Act of 1986 endorsed those principles mentioned. The main decisions were that preventive rather than curative action should be taken over pollution, that environmental damage should be rectified at source, and that the polluter must pay the costs of prevention and rectification. The SEA included the phrase that 'environmental protection requirements shall be a component of the Community's other policies'. This could be regarded as simply a bland form of words but the Act also said that any future Commission proposals about health, environmental protection and consumer protection would 'take as a base a high level of protection'. This partly explains the wide-ranging measures and disputes over environmental policy that have emerged since 1986.

The concept that 'the polluter must pay' is frequently voiced. It sounds clear, straightforward and just. In practice, however, it is by no means simple. It is not always easy to identify a polluter although scientific tests are improving so much that it is now possible to identify the origins of most oil spillages. Even then it is not always easy to identify the spiller. Atmospheric pollution cannot always be traced to its source. Moreover, there is a code of legal practice for waste disposal. People often exceed these legal limits in an undetected or accidental fashion. Even water authorities are sometimes forced to pollute waterways with excessively toxic levels of discharge. There is also a major disagreement sometimes about the safe level of pollutant or discharge. One of the functions of the Community policy is to fix standards of emissions, discharges and additives.

Who should pay to protect the environment?

The phrase 'the polluter should pay' frequently means, in practice, that the consumer pays in the form of higher prices. This is the case with water supplies, emissions from power station flues and car exhaust controls. If the supplier is a 'natural monopolist', as with water and electricity, most of the burden of increased cleanliness is passed on to the consumer. If the industry is oligopolistic, as with petroleum, then most of the burden will be borne by the consumer but its extent will depend on the effectiveness of the collusion among sellers.

The principle of the polluter paying may depend upon the state creating a very effective inspection, supervision and monitoring service backed by effective punishment for malpractice. Most of the costs of this will fall on the taxpayer because the regulatory system, if effective as a deterrent, will produce insufficient income to pay for itself. The principle eventually boils down to the fact that an industry has to pay for any of the costs needed to equip itself to comply with minimum standards. The knowledge that these costs will be passed on to consumers partly explains the reluctance of United Kingdom ministers before 1988 to order the Central Electricity Generating Board to spend nearly £2 billion on further cleansing of coal-powered power stations' flue gases. A classic instance of the consumer bearing the costs of improvements in the quality of life is illustrated in the statement by the United Kingdom Secretary of State for the Environment, in March 1989, that it would cost £2400 million to improve the quality of Britain's drinking and bathing water and to bring sewerage systems up to a standard to comply with existing Community directives. He estimated that this would add between $7\frac{1}{2}$ and 12 per cent to the capital costs of the water industry over the next decade.

The alternative to the consumer paying is for the government to cover some costs out of taxation. Another possibility is to identify the polluter and make him pay. At present, many 'polluters' are undetected. They are, in effect, keeping their production costs down by not having effluent or emission control and treatment. They are managing to make someone else pay some of their costs in terms of dirt, noise, unusable land, dead rivers and plant life, or dead animals. These costs are called 'external' costs by economists and are foisted on to the community at large or in particular. Occasionally, there can be external benefits when a firm improves the environment and reduces other people's costs or raises the quality of their lives. The result of the existence of these external costs and benefits means that there is often a divergence between the private and social costs of an economic activity. It may be profitable in terms of private costs and revenues alone. But if externalities are taken into account the deficit between social costs and benefits may outweigh the private profit. That is to say, that the private firm is profitable commercially but society as a whole is losing more than the firm's private profit.

The Community has recognised this fact and has implemented a directive which says that major public or private development projects in agriculture, industry or infrastructure (e.g. road building) must produce an environmental impact assessment before the work begins. The instigator must analyse potential pollution or other impact such as noise, on soil, air and water. The effects on wildlife habitats must also be considered. Permission for the project is only granted, and then possibly with conditions attached, after these environmental considerations have been balanced against the social, economic and other benefits of the scheme.

The United Kingdom's Role in the Community 9

The United Kingdom's role in the European Community is greater than would be indicated by a study of objective factors such as population, GDP per head and growth rates alone. In population size the United Kingdom is behind West Germany and Italy and only slightly ahead of France. The United Kingdom's GDP in 1987 was the sixth largest in the world behind the USA, Japan, USSR, West Germany and France but its GDP per head was eighteenth in the world ranking. In the Community, Luxembourg, Denmark, West Germany, France, the Netherlands and, arguably, Italy, had higher GDPs per head than Britain. The United Kingdom's growth rates, with rare exceptional periods, have also been lower. It is possible, if you choose your base date carefully, to argue that her growth rate in the 1980s has been the highest in Europe, but that involves a comparison from a very low starting point. Other measures such as the provision of health, welfare and social security services also put Britain fairly low in the league.

Despite these objective factors, however, the United Kingdom has assumed a very important role in the Community and has frequently set the political agenda and the pace of change. In many fields such as technological and scientific research programmes, monetary reforms, tax harmonisation and the removal of customs barriers, the United Kingdom has acted as a sort of drag anchor. It has had the same effect on most environmental proposals such as those to control atmospheric pollution and exhaust emissions, although there have been some signs of a change in attitude in 1989.

Why Has Britain's Policy Been So Negative?

It is very difficult to find any area in which the United Kingdom has been in the forefront of constructive change and where it has generated general support from the other members. It has, however, frequently allied itself with one or other of the other leading members in order to frustrate change, even if its motives are very different from those of its fellow objector. This approach, which is seen essentially as one of national self-interest, has sometimes led continental observers to recommend that the United Kingdom leave the Community because its thinking is not 'European'. These observers recognise that other members, particularly France, also act in a narrowly self-interested fashion from time to time, but they assert that the United Kingdom persistently acts in this way to the long-term detriment of the Community.

There are many possible reasons for this negative, obstructionist attitude on the part of the United Kingdom. One is an innate sense of Anglo-Saxon superiority which may be completely unjustified but is hard to shift. This may create an attitude of contempt and suspicion for continental methods and solutions. It is bolstered by the national mythology that is absorbed in place of modern history in the British educational system and which is perpetuated by the majority of the media. This ill-informed chauvinism may be excusable in the mass of the less well educated population but is inexcusable in the governing and opinion forming groups. It could be argued that despite the enormous improvements in transport and communications, the 'establishment', or governing classes, are less cosmopolitan or international in outlook and experience than their predecessors of the nineteenth and eighteenth centuries.

One of the more worrying aspects of this sense of Anglo-Saxon superiority is that it seems to prevent an objective appraisal of the relative successes and failures of initiatives and policies which have originated in the member states. One might have expected, for example, that the undoubted success of the West German economic and social policies would have led British policy-makers to emulate them. Perhaps the success of continental urban transport systems or of, say, the French regional planning, deserves more attention. The British have traditionally boasted of their pragmatic or empirical approach and scorned the supposed methods of philosophic, intellectual, rational argument from first principles adopted by continentals. But pragmatism may quickly dissolve into a confused and tangled muddle with conflicting and non-cohesive policies. The emphasis on *ad hoc* solutions to problems is inherent in the British system of administration. It has produced ineffective and over-lapping bureaucracy. A case in point was the overlap between education, as administered by the Department of Education and Science, and training which was largely influenced by the Training Commission and run by the Department of Trade and Industry. The structure of British government creates great problems of liaison and consultation between departments. Delays inevitably accompany this process.

Another cause of the United Kingdom's rather negative approach to many European proposals has been the baleful influence of pressure groups. Until 1988, say, or 1985 depending on how you interpret the evidence, the National Farmers' Union had a powerful influence on British policy in the context of the CAP. The same can be argued about all the farming lobbies in Europe, but the British lobby gave the impression of being a puppeteer pulling the strings with the Minister of Agriculture as the puppet. Similarly, the United Kingdom vehicle manufacturers seem to have exerted enormous influence on ministers in persuading them to go for a low level of targets for the control of vehicle exhaust emissions. The power generators and those who put large volumes of pollutants into the atmosphere also helped to set low targets and postponed dates for the targets that were agreed. The water supply industry dragged its feet over cleaning up water and beaches, although it can be argued that this was because the government would not permit it to invest sufficiently in improvements. In each case the British consumer will suffer in the long run through higher prices and has suffered in the short run from inferior products and pollution. In addition, the United Kingdom has incurred much displeasure among our more forward-looking partners in the Community.

Another probable cause of the United Kingdom's negative approach to many Community programmes is the fact that it, more than any other member, has extensive international, extra-European, political and economic links. There is still an extensive trading and commercial link with the Commonwealth. There is also a heavier commitment to the North Atlantic alliance and a deeper involvement in the Far East and central and southern Africa. The United Kingdom is also more important, relatively, as the site for foreign investment, particularly North American, Japanese and Middle Eastern. Until the entry of Spain and Portugal whose languages are used in South and Central America, the United Kingdom was unrivalled in the influence it exerted through its linguistic links. The United Kingdom remains important because of the use of English as the major language of commerce, science and literature.

It may be that Britain's tendency to obstructionist policies is a temporary phenomenon which will pass with the eventual demise of 'Thatcherism'. On the whole, the free market, enterprise culture emphasis of Thatcherite economics is incompatible with the long-term prevailing tenor of the Community. This accepts and recommends liberalisation of individuals, institutions and trade within a positive interventionist framework of controls. Such an approach has generally been highly successful. It developed, of course, to counteract exactly those evils of the free market which the proponents of Thatcherism have conveniently forgotten existed. The mature, coalition type, consensus-seeking governments of Europe have learned the great lesson of human society that cooperation achieves more in the long run than aggression, conflict and confrontation. It is highly unlikely that the efficient, effective and popular social democratic governments of the majority of European states will be supplanted by *laissez-faire*, free marketeer supporters. Indeed, the upsurge of 'green' or environmentalist parties demonstrates the opposite trend.

What Have Been the Attitudes of the British Press to the Community?

There is very little coverage of the day-to-day workings of the Community in the popular press. It covers summit meetings in general terms and sometimes takes up an issue or proposal in more depth. The newspapers which are generally 'anti' favour those stories that seem to put the Community in a bad light. Some of these are scare stories such as the threat to the King Edward potato or to the mile, or similar themes thought to be close to the heart of the readership. Occasionally, the stories would be of conflicts such as those with 'unreasonable' French farmers who did not want our exports of lamb or Spanish exports of fruit. The general effect has been to portray the Community as something alien run by odd foreign bureaucrats. The greatest amount of space has probably been devoted to the agricultural policies and food 'mountains'. Since the Single European Act was passed an increasing number of articles have been about threatened uniformity, the problems of border controls and terrorists or rabies, and harmonisation of taxation. Some of the prompting for these stories appears to have come from the unattributable lobby briefings to parliamentary journalists. That is to say, they are prompted by the British government.

The Channel Tunnel has provoked an interesting conflict of opinion. After all the initial anti statements about it being unnecessary, dangerous and unlikely to happen, the press began to say what a wonderful feat of British civil engineering it would be. Then the problems of liaison with the French and border inspections aroused interest. Some tried to portray it as a race. Then the anti feelings surfaced as the Kent population protested against the new high speed railway link. Now, gradually, the United Kingdom is coming under very heavy criticism for failing to plan improvements in the rail links to the regions so that they too may benefit from the tunnel. In contrast to the rest of the Community the United Kingdom's investment in railway modernisation is seen as inadequate. As the road system, and particularly the M25, is revealed as grossly inadequate and badly planned, more people are looking with admiration at our continental counterparts' foresight and effectiveness in planning and subsidising their own networks.

There are signs that the popular press is beginning to lose its knee jerk response to Community proposals. It no longer automatically castigates them as harmful to Britain. Indeed, it has welcomed some proposals particularly in the environmental sphere. It has given a general welcome to the European passport and driving licence. There are, however, many pitfalls ahead, such as the probable abolition of duty free facilities for intra-Community travel and the final effective metrication of old imperial measures. Such changes will undoubtedly rouse the chauvinist lion lurking in the editorial offices of the British press.

The so called 'quality' press also devotes remarkably little space to European matters although this is gradually changing as 1992 approaches. There is thorough coverage of summit meetings and of some Council meetings, and there are regular correspondents in Brussels and Strasbourg who keep track of weekly events – and who often feel the need to put a humorous gloss on their reporting. The City pages contain an increasing number of references to Community affairs and fairly frequent special studies. There is undoubtedly a growing awareness of the importance of the Community and a dawning realisation that the centre of power and decision-making is gradually shifting away from London. These changes are also taking place on television programmes devoted to current events of a political or economic nature. Both newspapers and television are, of course, targeted by the public relations officers of the European Community and of the Parliament.

Has the United Kingdom Gained from Membership?

The economist often talks about 'opportunity cost'. This is the cost, in financial terms, of the next best alternative foregone if a particular course of action is chosen. If the United Kingdom chooses to spend £9 billion on a missile system there is an opportunity cost involved of the other things that could have been bought with the money – roads, schools, hospitals, aircraft or pay rises for MPs. In the case of the United Kingdom's membership of the European Community it is very hard to measure the opportunity cost of membership. Nobody can tell accurately what would have happened to the economy if the United Kingdom had not joined. Some argue that its future would have been rosier and that like Norway, for example, the United Kingdom would have done very well outside the Community. They point to the undoubted accumulated net contribution to the Community over the years to 1984, although the exact figure is hard to quantify. They see that as money wasted. They see the Common Agricultural Policy as an unnecessary expense that has placed a considerable extra burden on every household every year. Some place this figure as high as an extra £300 per household per year in the 1980s.

Against this net outflow, which is not accurately quantifiable, must be set the gains from the Regional and Social Funds. The United Kingdom received almost £2 billion from the Regional Development Fund between 1975 and the end of 1987. Large sums have also been received from the Social Fund, £400 million in 1988 alone. These sums have mainly benefited the areas of high unemployment but not exclusively so. Some governments have used these inflows to cut their own taxation revenues allocated to regional assistance. But what is hardest to measure is the gain from trade arising from the large common market. Although this will not be a true 'single' market until after 1992, the gains from specialisation, economies of scale and the incentives to greater competitive efficiency have been very large. The gains to the commercial and financial sectors have also been extensive. There have, however, been casualties and many firms and individuals have suffered materially from the greater competitiveness of some European firms. The peripheries have sometimes been hardest hit and there is a tendency for the central wealth generating 'power house' of the Community to lie in the Ile de France, the Benelux countries and north-western Germany, with an overlap into southern England. Economic geographers pay a great deal of attention to monitoring the growth of this region.

There is a major gain to all members in terms of the mutual help given to less favoured regions and the assistance given to cushion declining industries. This redistributive aspect is not welcomed by all. There is also a major gain to all in the fields of scientific and technological research cooperation. Although these programmes do not compare in scale with Japanese and American expenditures, they are beginning to make inroads into the research backlog and permit competition in selected areas.

There was little attraction in the long-term economic or political future for the United Kingdom outside the European Community. The old Commonwealth ties were weakening, the new Commonwealth ties were fairly feeble and the preferential trading system was in decline. Economic stagnation brought military and political impotence. The political influence of the United Kingdom faded as the imperial grandeur receded and the new economic might of the United States was displayed. Eventually, Britain's leaders have recognised this. One of the most encouraging developments in the Community in the late 1980s has been the trend towards concerted political influence in, for example, southern Africa, the Middle East and international financial organisations such as the United Nations. The Community may not be many years away from having a single foreign policy on many issues or areas.

On balance, therefore, the United Kingdom may or may not be out of pocket financially as a result of membership. There is no doubt, however, that it is stronger both economically and politically than if it had remained outside. There are signs too that the people of the United Kingdom will increasingly have to look to Europe and its Court of Justice for protection of basic rights and freedoms. The idea that some people have of leaving the Community is unrealistic nonsense based on a romanticised view of British history and an overoptimistic assessment of the future. There might be a sort of half-way house as an associate member but that would be less viable after the 1992 single market becomes fully effective.

The United Kingdom and the European Parliament

The European Parliament was called the 'Assembly' in the treaties establishing the Community. Until 1979 the members (MEPs) were appointed from their national parliaments. The appointments were, of course, related to party strengths. The original treaties had intended members to be elected but disagreements among the Six prevented this happening until after the accession of the United Kingdom, Denmark and Ireland in 1973. Even so, the first British MEPs were appointed not elected. In the election of 1979 410 MEPs were elected to the Parliament. This number rose to 518 after the accession of Greece in 1981 and Portugal and Spain in 1986. The elections are held every five years – 1979, 1984, 1989, and so on. The number of MEPs per country is based broadly on population but not as exactly as, say, the United States electoral districts for Congressional elections. The intention of the European Parliament since 1982 has been that the elections should be by a regionally based system of proportional representation. This was intended to improve the chances of election of all but tiny parties. The member states did not agree and the 1984 election was held with a mixture of systems according to country. They also failed to agree for the 1989 election. The United Kingdom has proved a major stumbling block to agreement. Britain's main parties have a vested interest in retaining the archaic first past the post method of election. It enables them to exclude other parties, even those with a significant measure of support. In an act of condescension, however, they graciously permit the people of Northern Ireland to elect three MEPs in a single constituency by the version of proportional representation known as the Single Transferable Vote (STV). The STV is used in Northern Ireland local elections and in Ireland's parliamentary elections.

England has 66 MEPs, Scotland 8, Wales 4 and Northern Ireland 3, making a total for the United Kingdom of 81.

In 1979, the Conservatives had 60 and Labour 17 European Parliament seats.

In 1984, the Conservatives had 45 and Labour 32 European Parliament seats.

In 1989, the Conservatives had 32 and Labour 45 European Parliament seats. The Scottish Nationalist Party had 1 seat. The 3 Northern Ireland seats were Official Unionist, Democratic Unionist, and Social Democratic and Labour (see Table 9.1).

The United Kingdom, France, Germany and Italy each have 81 MEPs, despite their population differences. Spain has 60, the Netherlands 25, Belgium, Greece and Portugal 24 each, Denmark 16, Ireland 15 and Luxembourg 6 (see Table 9.2 and Figure 9.1).

TABLE 9.1
Results of the June 1989 Elections for the European Parliament

GREAT BRITAIN

	Votes	%	Seats
Labour	6 153 604	40.12	45
Conservative	5 224 037	34.15	32
Green	2 292 705	14.99	—
SLD	986 292	6.44	—
SNP	406 686	2.65	1
Plaid Cymru	115 062	0.75	—
SDP	75 886	0.49	—
Others	39 971	0.30	—
	15 294 243	100	78

Electorate: 42 590 060
Turnout: 35.91%

TABLE 9.1 *cont.*

NORTHERN IRELAND

	First preference	%	Seats
Paisley, Ian (Democratic Unionist)	160 110	29.94	1
Hume, John (Social Dem and Lab)	136 335	25.49	1
Nicholson, Jim (Official Unionist)	118 785	22.21	1
Morrison, Danny (Sinn Fein)	48 914	9.15	—
Alderdice, John (Alliance)	27 905	5.22	—
Kennedy, Lawrence (Nth Down Con)	25 789	4.83	—
Samuel, M. H. (Green)	6 569	1.23	—
Lynch, S. (Workers')	5 590	1.04	—
Langhammer, Mark (Lab Rep in N.I.)	3 540	0.66	—
Caul, B. (Lab 87)	1 274	0.24	—
Total	534 811	100	3

Turnout: 47.7%   Electorate: 1 120 508

● Elections in Northern Ireland are conducted under a system of proportional representation, using the single transferable vote in a three-member constituency.

SOURCE   *European Parliament News*, July 1989.

What Impact Have the United Kingdom's MEPs Made?

Before the enlargement of the Community after 1972 the European Parliament was a rather innocuous, largely powerless talking shop. The British press, rather arrogantly, assumed that the introduction of British MEPs would be like taking the light of the gospel of parliamentary democracy to the benighted heathen. They ignored, of course, the extent to which the United Kingdom Parliament had, in the words of Enoch Powell and Tony Benn, become 'craven' –

TABLE 9.2

Further Results of the June 1989 Elections for the European Parliament

	B	Dk	G	Gr	S	F	Irl	I	L	N	P	UK	12
Soc	8	4	31	9	27	22	1	14	2	8	8	46	180
EPP	7	2	32	10	16	6	4	27	3	10	3	1	121
LDR	4	3	4	—	6	13	2	3	1	4	9	—	49
ED	—	2	—	—	—	—	—	—	—	—	—	32	34
Greens	3	—	8	—	1	8	—	7	—	2	1	—	30
EUL	—	1	—	1	4	—	—	22	—	—	—	—	28
EDA	—	—	—	1	—	13	6	—	—	—	—	—	20
ER	1	—	6	—	—	10	—	—	—	—	—	—	17
LU	—	—	—	3	—	7	1	—	—	—	3	—	14
RBW	1	4	—	—	2	1	1	3	—	—	—	1	13
Ind	—	—	—	—	4	1	—	5	—	1	—	1	12
Totals	24	16	81	24	60	81	15	81	6	25	24	81	518

Abbreviations: Soc: Socialist Group. EPP: Group of the European People's Party (Christian-Democratic Group). LDR: Liberal Democratic and Reformist Group. ED: European Democratic Group. Greens: Group of the Greens in the European Parliament. EUL: Group of the European United Left. EDA: Group of the European Democratic Alliance. ER: Technical Group of the European Right. LU: Left Unity. RBW: Rainbow Group. Ind: Non-attached. B: Belgium. Dk: Denmark. F: France. G: Germany. Gr: Greece. I: Italy. Irl: Ireland. L: Luxembourg. N: Netherlands. P: Portugal. S: Spain. UK: United Kingdom.

SOURCE   *European Parliament News*, July 1989.

that is, the feeble rubber stamp to the proposals of the government of the day. Much was made of the introduction of the more extensive use of 'questions' in the European Parliament. This extra use of questions for both written and oral reply by the responsible people has greatly benefited the MEPs in their role as democratic guardians. Each question is inordinately expensive to answer, though,

FIGURE 9.1
The European Parliament July, 1989

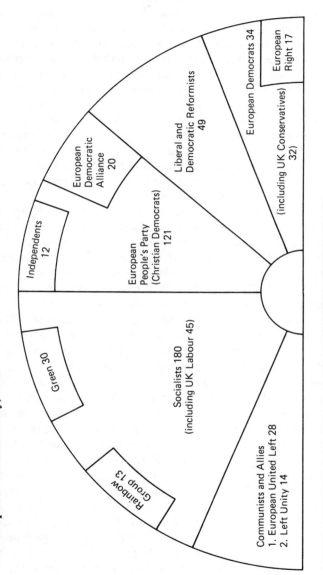

because of the translation and printing costs associated with replies. Questions in the British House of Commons are also very expensive to answer. In Britain, Question Time, especially on Tuesday and Thursday when the Prime Minister answers a tiny number of questions, is seen as a forum for the gladiatorial nature of confrontational politics. Its impact and effectiveness is grossly overrated except for rare moments of historical importance. The European question sessions are more constructive, genuinely seek information and clarification and usually have less crudely political motivation. This is mainly because the Parliament is not a bipartisan confrontational assembly but a shifting series of alliances. It is also because the 'audience', the electorate, is not usually informed on a daily basis of the doings of the European Parliament and there is no need to play to the gallery of public opinion.

One major impact of the advent of the United Kingdom MEPs was the introduction of English as the major language, with French, for communication. English had often been the only common language of MEPs and was in frequent use but its introduction as an official language raised its status, availability and use.

United Kingdom MEPs have usually operated as fairly tightly 'whipped' blocks. They consult together, plan coordinated approaches and decide voting tactics and strategies. They try to maintain constant alliances with like-minded groups from other nations. The Conservative MEPs have been particularly active in reflecting the wishes of the home leadership of the national party in the issues being debated in relation to the single market. The European Parliament sometimes tends to be dominated by left of centre and centre coalitions with a preference for social democracy and interventionism. The United Kingdom Conservative MEPs have been very active in opposing these principles. Occasionally, they have been the only group apart from the European right to vote against measures proposed by the Commission. Sometimes the Parliament is dominated by centre and centre-right groups.

It is difficult to separate the effects of the advent of United Kingdom members from those resulting from the introduction of elected representatives and the passing of the Single European Act which extended the European Parliament's power. On the whole, most of the changes seem to have stemmed from the fact that members are elected instead of appointed. Elections have given MEPs greater confidence and independence, and this has been reflected in the growing willingness of Parliament to confront the Commission and criticise proposals of both it and the Council of Ministers. Parliament has begun to propose an increasing number of ideas for legislation on its own initiative. The Commission has acted on most of these. It is evident that MEPs are increasingly concerned at the failure of the Council of Ministers to agree on measures that have already been approved by Parliament. Indeed, the European Parliament has taken the Council of Ministers to the European Court of Justice for failing to implement a transport policy which the Parliament had approved. This event is of very great long-term importance because it shows that the European Parliament could develop into a highly effective and democratic force.

It is slightly ironic that United Kingdom MEPs have been very active and articulate over budgetary matters in the European Parliament, since the United Kingdom Parliament has largely lost its budgetary functions and endorses executive and Treasury proposals. The opposition in the House of Commons rarely achieves any change in the budget on taxation proposals or in the estimates for expenditure. Government backbenchers may achieve minor changes in committee if the government approves. The European Parliament, in contrast, has the right to reject the Commission's budget and has done so twice in 1979 and 1984. The European Parliament's Budgetary Control Committee is also more effective than the House of Commons equivalents. It checks the ways in which money is spent and can ask the Court of Auditors to carry out special enquiries. The court may advise the Parliament to refuse to accept the annual accounts if it is not satisfied. As a generalisation the British House of Commons' financial control is, in contrast, patchy, inexpert, ineffective and delayed. Generally, it is a case of 'closing the stable door after the horse has bolted'.

The Committees of the Parliament

The eighteen permanent committees of the European Parliament are at the root of its work. Their membership is reasonably representative of the strength of the political groupings within the Parliament and their meetings are frequently attended by Commissioners and officials. Public hearings are held at which specialists and experts give evidence; some of these are, of course, pressure groups. The

Parliament debates the committees' reports and may amend their recommendations before they are sent back to the Commission which then presents them to the Council for final decision. On most matters it is legally necessary to obtain the Parliament's opinion before legislation can be made. Most of the committee meetings are held in Brussels but some are held elsewhere, even in member countries.

The Committees in 1989 were: Political; Agriculture, Fisheries, Food and Rural Development; Budgets; Economic, Monetary, Industrial; Energy, Research, Technology; External Economic Relations; Legal, Citizen's Rights; Social and Employment and Working Environment; Regional Policy and Planning; Transport and Tourism; Environment, Health and Consumer Affairs; Overseas Development and Cooperation; Budgetary Control; Procedure, Petitions; Women's Rights; Institutional Affairs; Members' Credentials; and Youth, Culture, Education, Information, Sport. This list gives an insight into the difference of attitude and interests of the European Parliament compared with that of the United Kingdom. In the House of Commons the emphasis is on committees which 'shadow' departments and their work. There are, for example, environmental and transport departmental select committees. But things like women's rights, or youth, or culture, have to take a place at the back of the queue in the select committees' deliberations. They are not seen as important enough to have their own committee.

The impact of the United Kingdom Euro MPs has, therefore, been significant but it has not been in the nature of the transformation from darkness to light that was originally predicted. Indeed, over the next few years, especially if proportional representation is adopted throughout the Community, more and more people will see the European Parliament as the true centre of effective democracy and the main protection of individual liberties. A national Parliament such as the United Kingdom's will appear to have diminished in relevance and importance. This may be less true in some European countries where their electoral system, party systems and parliamentary procedures have been updated. The United Kingdom, with its increasingly unrepresentative Parliament, its archaic structures, its executive dominated legislature, its unelected second chamber and its lack of explicit protection for the individual's rights, will inevitably suffer in comparison.

The United Kingdom and the Commission

The Commission is the executive of the Community and is, supposedly, independent of the national governments. It answers to the European Parliament for its initiation and execution of policy. The Commission has seventeen members, two each from the United Kingdom, France, Italy, Germany and Spain and one each from the others. The President, chosen in 1985, is Jacques Delors who has proved to be particularly dynamic. The members of the Commission are appointed for four years by national governments and then distribute their responsibilities among themselves. In the United Kingdom, the government nominates one and the opposition the other. In practice, the opposition's nominee needs to be acceptable to the Prime Minister. Commissioners, once appointed, are intended to be completely independent of their national governments. This makes it essential from the government's point of view that the people chosen have attitudes which will not lead to a sacrifice of national self-interest. The Commission has become a vital power base in Europe and its President has an important relationship to the Heads of Government of Community members. For example, the President, M. Delors, has on several occasions antagonised Mrs Thatcher on the subject of European unity, monetary union, trade union affairs and a European central bank.

A new group of Commissioners began work in January 1989. Mrs Thatcher thought that her previous Commissioner, Lord Cockfield, who had been Vice President of the Commission in charge of the progress towards the Single Market, had 'gone native'. She opposed his reappointment and that of the other United Kingdom Commissioner, Mr Stanley Clinton Davis, who had the portfolio for environment, nuclear safety and transport. The United Kingdom Commissioners appointed in January 1989 were Sir Leon Brittan, in charge of competition policy and financial institutions, and Bruce Millan, in charge of regional policy.

The United Kingdom and the Council of Ministers

The Council of Ministers sometimes comprises the twelve finance ministers of the members, or the twelve agriculture ministers, or the twelve transport ministers, and so on. The Presidency of the Council changes every six months. The next turn for the United Kingdom will be the second half of 1992. These meetings lay down the Community policy and the important decisions must be unanimous although many may be by a qualified majority of 54 votes out of a total of 74. The ministers are there to act as spokesmen but the real work is done by their civil servants. The meetings have had a reputation for brinkmanship and making decisions only at the very last possible moment. These gatherings usually receive very slender treatment in the press but are frequently of major, long-term importance. The Council has a committee to service it called COREPER or the Committee of Permanent Representatives. These are the ambassadors of the members to the Community and their advisers.

In addition, at least twice a year, there is a meeting of the European Council which is attended by the Heads of Government; foreign ministers also attend to give background advice. The President of the Commission is another participant. These so called summits have sometimes had enormous influence in shifting the path of the Community towards new objectives. The system of each member having a six-month stint acting as President of the Council of Ministers leads to beneficial shifts of emphasis. Some periods are highly productive in new ideas whereas others largely consolidate past efforts. The meetings are a welcome media event for the national leaders who can be seen acting as their nation's champions, in company with their equals or more powerful neighbours. Such division as occurs is played down by the public relations machine and each leader's point of view is presented in its best light for home consumption. If the divisions have been deep and real the final communiqué will be rather bland and non-committal. It may be couched in what is often called 'eurospeak' which is a mixture of fine sounding phrases capable of several interpretations and technical jargon which gives new terminology to ideas and policies. Examples include extensification, harmonisation, set-aside, and a whole range of initials. Many of the words are already in the new edition of the *Oxford English Dictionary*. There is also a dictionary called *Eurojargon* written by Anne Ramsay (Capital Planning Information, 52 High Street, St Martin's, Stamford, Lincs, PE9 2LG, £12.50). It is already in its second edition (1989), and its contents have risen from

850 to 1400 entries. Some of the 'eurospeak' words are simply French words for which there is no straightforward translation, some are acronyms and others are invented. No one has taken much notice of the desire of the Esperanto Society to have esperanto made an official language of the Community!

The Future and the Single Market 10

What Alternative Policies for Development Are There?

Some see the future of the Community as an expanding free trade area with the emphasis on free markets, the mobility of factors of production, labour capital and enterprise, and a legal framework that regulates commerce and trade with the minimum of hindrance. They stress the 'market of 320 million people', economies of scale, position to influence international affairs and the maintenance of distinctive national customs and culture. They support the policies put forward in the Single European Act because they see the completion of the internal market as realising their hopes.

Others see a European Community of the future as one without trade barriers, without hindrance to the mobility of factors, with the economies of scale but with a legal framework that encourages the harmonisation of standards and has a major social dimension. They envisage a more interventionist approach, a more positive direction through regulation, expenditure and taxation to achieve social goals such as lower unemployment or decreased poverty. They see the Community as essentially an economic union which has a major social role.

There are others who go further and look forward to a deeper and more far-reaching political union. They see the economic harmonisation leading inexorably towards some more concrete political union such as a federal states of Europe. This concept has already

166

been discussed. Their expectation is that initially the ECU will appear as an additional European currency used by those who find it convenient but that it will eventually replace all the individual national currencies. Some predict that this might be as early as 1995. At the same time, progress would be made to the establishment of a European central bank to administer the common monetary policy and to regulate the foreign exchange value of the ECU. They think that even if initially some taxes are not harmonised the long-run pressures will be towards harmonisation. If, for example, France or the United Kingdom maintain different VAT rates there will be a tendency to cross-border buying which will force governments into equalising rates. This principle would, they allege, apply in many areas of economic activity if differences are maintained.

These supporters of deeper political union are already pointing to the development of united Community foreign policy initiatives in relation to Third World issues, to Namibia and southern Africa, to Iran and the Salman Rushdie affair, and to united action against terrorism. The Community is increasingly seeking to put a collective voice in the United Nations and the International Monetary Fund. There is a growing interest, or rebirth of interest, in the idea of a collective European defence force and its possible replacement of NATO. The French and Germans are already operating a joint battalion of troops as an experiment. Such people may be too optimistic about the time-scale of political union, but it is difficult to see how the creation of a truly integrated economic community of 320 million people can fail to generate pressure for greater political union.

The above points need to be seen against the changing political climate in Eastern Europe where there are signs, under Mr Gorbachev, of a fundamental shift of Soviet foreign and defence policies. Another factor is the desire of the United States to reduce its colossal balance of payments deficit and to cut the costs of its NATO commitment. Although the political and economic situation in several of the Warsaw Pact countries, and in some of the states of the USSR, is increasingly unstable, the medium-term prospect is for reduced levels of conventional and nuclear forces on the East–West border in Europe. This will call into question the continued need for NATO and the American commitment to defend Europe with land forces. It will place greater emphasis on the sense of a European Community defence policy and a united foreign policy for dealing with its neighbours. Such a unified policy would make the entry of neutral Austria and Sweden into the Community more difficult.

The Single European Act

In 1985, the Heads of Government asked the Commission to put forward proposals to achieve a fully unified internal market by the end of 1992. The Commission produced a White Paper in June 1985 which set out a programme and timetable for action. The Heads of Government accepted the proposals at their meeting in Luxembourg in December 1985. The Single European Act incorporating the decisions was signed in February 1986 and came into force on 1 July 1987. It had taken thirty years from the Treaty of Rome to reach the decision to complete a genuine, unified market.

The aims of the Single European Act

At its simplest the aims are to do what the Treaty of Rome originally intended. That treaty begins: 'Determined to lay the foundations of an ever closer union among the peoples of Europe. Resolved to ensure the economic and social progress of their countries by common action to eliminate the barriers which divide Europe.' In practice, many of the barriers remained. They were physical, technical and fiscal in nature. Some had simply never been removed; others had been created or strengthened to protect national or sectional self-interest. Looked at closely the Community was rarely a single, unified market. More often it remained a series of separate, national markets.

As a result the main aim is to remove the remaining obstacles to the free movement of people, goods and services. These consist of a great variety of different national technical specifications, health and safety regulations, quality controls and environmental standards. Added to these is a formidable array of legislative differences relating to companies, financial markets, banking, direct and indirect taxes. It is possible to get a good idea of the extent of these obstacles from the Department of Trade and Industry's information package called 'The Single Market – the Facts'. This is regularly updated and is distributed free to all interested businesses and persons. A very detailed analysis of the costs of not having a unified market is contained in *The European Challenge, 1992: The Benefits of a Single Market* by Paolo Cecchini (published by Wildwood House for the European Commission). His research revealed the colossal cost of what is now called 'non-Europe'.

What Are the Costs of a 'Non-Europe'?

The cost of not having a genuine unified market can be measured in terms of the inefficient use of resources, leading to extra costs being imposed on the taxpayer and consumer. These costs could be reduced if the market were improved.

The research had to make some assumptions which could, no doubt, be challenged in some respects. Its main conclusion is that the total economic gain from the completion of the internal market would be the equivalent of about 5 per cent of the Community's Gross Domestic Product – about 200 billion ECU at 1988 prices. This figure includes savings from the removal of barriers to intra-Community trade (border formalities and delays), together with the benefits from the removal of obstacles to entry to different national markets, and from an end to restrictions on competition.

Another indication of the research was that the medium-term effect of creating a single internal market would be the lowering of consumer prices by about 6 per cent. At the same time, output, employment and living standards would rise. The number of new jobs created would be between 2 and 5 million depending on what macroeconomic policies were adopted. The savings from increased economies of scale for manufacturing industries were estimated at 2 per cent of the GDP of the Community. Some sectors might gain cost reductions of only 1 per cent but others might gain 7 per cent.

These figures of cost reductions and net potential gains are very impressive. However, there would be other less quantifiable gains arising from greater freedom to move about Europe for work or leisure, and a greater competitive capacity in international markets compared with Japan and the USA.

What Physical Barriers Need to Be Removed?

The physical barriers concerned are mainly immigration controls and customs. When the single market is completed there will still be immigration controls on people from outside the Community. At present, the frontier controls on Community citizens are aimed at checking passports or identity cards to prevent illegal immigration and to check that taxation has been paid. Since 1967 the barriers at internal frontiers have not been customs posts and the phrase has not been used since January 1988 on internal borders. There are a variety of different levels of checking at these internal frontiers depending on whether the mode of transport is road, rail or air. At one extreme there may be no regular check; at the other there may be a full computerised record made of entry. The intention is to remove all controls at the internal frontiers of the Community by 1992 by means of a gradual relaxation. It will be necessary to end the system of controls which ensure that VAT has been paid on goods being transferred between states by individuals. The harmonisation of VAT levels and regulations would make this easier.

The United Kingdom has expressed great concern about the removal of these controls because it sees them as essential to check the movement of criminals, drug traffickers and terrorists. Ireland and Denmark agree. The other members disagree and argue that the redundant internal border officials can be shifted to the external frontiers to make the outer perimeter more effective. They would also use frequent spot checks on internal borders. The United Kingdom is so adamant on this topic that it is going to build a special customs/immigration control at the Waterloo station terminal of the Channel Tunnel.

In contrast to the United Kingdom's reluctance to end border controls, five of the other members are anxious to end them in 1990 rather than wait for 1992. In March 1989, France, West Germany, Belgium, the Netherlands and Luxembourg produced a draft plan to introduce a border-free zone. Once free borders were introduced inside the zone they would create a stricter 'fence' around them to control immigration of non-Community nationals. Foreigners (non-EC nationals) would only require one visa to travel in all five countries. The draft agreement provides for special short-term border checks if national security or public order is at stake. This set of ideas is called the Schengen Group proposal and is likely to be the basis of the agreement reached for the whole Community for the end of 1992. One of the draft proposals is that the five countries should have a common political asylum policy. This has aroused the opposition of various Human Rights groups who think that the details are a breach of the Geneva Convention (1951).

Another main physical control concerns the movement of goods. These represent considerable and expensive delays, especially to commercial vehicles. The checks at borders have been for a variety of purposes, to collect taxes, obtain statistics, control plant and animal diseases, enforce trade quotas, reject banned goods, and to license some imports and exports. Major progress has already been made in removing some of these requirements. Since January 1988 there has been a Single Administrative Document for vehicles transporting goods across internal frontiers. This replaced about seventy separate forms. Many duplicate checks have also been eliminated and the intention is to remove any other inessential checks by 1992. These included some which date from the national quotas on steel production which were abolished in 1988. Other obstacles, such as agricultural and health controls, will be eliminated by harmonising policies so that there are no significant differences between national standards. Another major physical obstacle to be removed is the quota system on the number of journeys that foreign, or sometimes even national, hauliers can make. These quotas will be gradually relaxed and then abolished. It is in this context that the desire to raise the tonnage of motor vehicles from the present 38 tonnes to 42 is important, although it is axle loading which really matters. This removal of quotas will allow hauliers to operate freely throughout the Community and remove the need for frontier checks. There will, of course, have to be a new, common, set of safety standards for vehicles and consistency in their application and enforcement.

What Technical Barriers Need to Be Removed?

Even if all frontier barriers were removed there would still be a great hindrance to free trade because of the enormous variety of technical standards applied by each member state. Many of these differences relate to basic factors such as electrical voltages, wiring regulations, plumbing regulations and safety rules. Some relate to differing technical standards such as the three main colour television systems or the two video standards, VHS and Betamax (which is now being discontinued). A manufacturer of washing machines in the United

Kingdom might need to produce up to thirty slightly different versions of one model in order to satisfy all international markets. Most of the variations would relate to regulations about electrical wiring. The majority of manufacturers face similar problems. A classic example from the past was the temporary banning from the USA, on health grounds, of red Smarties. The red dye was alleged to have come from cochineal instead of 'healthier' chemical dyes.

Although some of these technical varieties are genuine and arise from historical developments, some are artificial and were introduced as a form of trade protection. The Germans, for example, have, to their great benefit, maintained the quality of their beer by keeping out foreign beers on the grounds that they contravened German food purity laws. Unfortunately, for German beer drinkers they are now forced to accept other Community members' beers containing carbon dioxide and other 'additives'.

All these differing technical standards impose considerable costs on producers. They reduce the available economies of scale and add significantly to research and development costs. Another effect is to hinder the development of Community-wide companies as it is easier for them to work within their own national boundaries.

Will Harmonisation Remove Technical Barriers?

The Community's early attempts at technical harmonisation may have done more harm than good in the attempt to impose elaborate and ambitious agreed standards. The idea was that everything in the Community should be uniform – Eurosausages, Europotatoes, etc. This approach was largely ineffective although it did achieve improvements such as tachographs in the cabs of commercial vehicles. Much more progress was made through the European Court of Justice. The most important single decision was made in 1979 in the Cassis de Dijon case which applied to the sale in Germany of cassis produced in France. The court ruled that there was a basic right of free movement of goods and that, in principle, goods legally manufactured in one member country could be sold in another. Thereafter, competing products from other members could not be precluded simply because they were slightly different, but only to protect consumer interests if the ban conformed to Community law.

Progress in removing technical barriers towards 1992 requires another approach towards harmonisation. This involves Community legislation which will only lay down mandatory requirements as general levels or standards of protection. The fixing of the details of their application will be left to European standardisation bodies. In addition, there will be some national rules which do not concern these requirements. Community legislation or harmonisation will not apply to them but they will be automatically subject to national mutual recognition which will be enforceable by the European Court of Justice. Such a system will prevent unnecessary harmonisation and will save a great deal of wrangling over detailed technical specifications.

There are, inevitably, some exceptions to this freer approach, mainly in high technology areas applicable to new developments and where operating standards must be the same, for example in telecommunications. Another major area is broadcasting, especially with satellites. The Community is adopting the 'MAC packet family' of standards which will help to create a Europe-wide audiovisual market and keep the Japanese at bay for longer. A set of common legal as well as technical standards is necessary and the financial gains from harmonisation in this sphere are enormous. The process of technical harmonisation partly explains the keenness of Japanese firms to establish themselves in the United Kingdom.

As the harmonisation process gradually takes effect there will be a noticeable impact on people's lives. New television sets already have 'euroconnection' ports on them. Computers and their printers may also have standardised connectors, plugs and sockets. Vehicle lights and exhaust emission control systems will meet the same European standards, and so on. Nevertheless, national diversity will remain. For example, the British 13 amp square pin plug and ring main system will remain for the foreseeable future.

Will We Have Harmonised 'Eurofood'?

People fear that local, regional or national foods will be squeezed out by food produced to harmonise European standards. This will not happen because members will be able to keep their own regulations on matters relating to health and safety. They will have to allow other members' products into their country provided that they match the country of origin's standards. The Community will simply ask for legislation guaranteeing that a food is fit to be eaten and that the labelling will give the purchaser full details of its contents. Once this is so the food can be sold anywhere in the Community.

Other Freedoms

The intention is to remove all physical restrictions on the movement of people within the Community. The main constraints at the moment are on the ability to study or work in other Community countries chiefly because of the lack of standards for educational qualifications, which are not always mutually recognised. This problem will be removed as the Commission is proposing the mutual recognition of higher education diplomas. This means that the student who has certain basic qualifications will be able to go freely anywhere in the Community to study. This might prove a godsend to British universities and colleges which are desperately anxious to attract foreign students who are able to pay.

There is an associated problem of the non-acceptability of vocational qualifications. The line of action being adopted by the Commission is to produce a 'vocational training card', the possession of which will mean that the owner has reached a certain generally accepted training standard and can seek work anywhere in the Community. This will have a major impact on training schemes and on labour mobility.

A similar problem of non-recognition of qualifications has existed for many years in respect of professional people and the self-employed in general. The old approach was to work laboriously towards directives. Much progress was made by this method in the health sector with a harmonised basic training for doctors, dentists, midwives and veterinary surgeons. This, with other regulations, has given them a 'right of establishment' and they can practice in all member states.

The use of directives has proved to be very cumbersome. It took seventeen years, for example, to agree directives to enable architects to practise anywhere they liked in the Community. In the run up to 1992 a new approach has been adopted by applying the 'Cassis de Dijon' principle again, whereby if a person is qualified to practise a vocation in one country of the Community then that person should, in principle, be able to practise it in another. The Community is therefore adopting the idea of a single system of mutual recognition which will apply to higher educational qualifications, leading to an entitlement to practise a vocation or profession. There may sometimes be a test of language comprehension in the area of expertise to be practised. However, it is very hard to predict the extent to which these changes will promote the movement of professional people, but there seems to be a growing tendency for architects to practise outside their own countries. This is, to some extent, a return to the days preceding official qualifications when architects practised wherever their clients wanted them.

One rather unusual application of the new principle will feature in a proposed European Charter for professional sportsmen, to be published in late 1989. This would guarantee their rights under social legislation and contain guidelines for the conditions of transfer of players between clubs. It has been suggested that the sale of players might be banned. This is speculation but it is hard to reconcile the transfer fee system as it applies in the United Kingdom with the European labour laws and its proposed revisions.

Capital and Financial Services

This subject has been dealt with in Chapter 7, but the freeing of the movement of capital is a very important step forward. The process may be delayed for Portugal and Spain in some respects. However, the aim is that, by the end of 1992, all financial transactions will be liberalised. Cash, bank transfers and any financial instrument will be freely transferable within the Community. There will also be some harmonisation of procedures for movement of capital to and from external countries. The initial directive is aimed at liberalising short-term operations – bills, certificates of deposit, current and deposit accounts, and loans and credits. The Commission intends keeping powers to reintroduce controls of short-term movements of capital if there is an emergency relating to foreign exchange rates.

Financial Services

The Treaty of Rome explicitly provided for the gradual abolition of restrictions on providing financial services, but relatively less has been achieved in this area than in the field of trade in goods. As a result there is a backlog of legislation to catch up on and some directives have been passed or are in the pipeline for 1992. These will liberalise the provision of several types of service such as banking, insurance, mortgages, securities, investment services and unit trusts. There is also a draft directive proposed which will legislate for insider dealing.

The Commission's aim is to leave as much as possible to be covered by the principle of mutual recognition, as in the harmonisation of trade in goods. It will try to restrict itself to controls which safeguard financial security and prudent practice. In every country there is already a great amount of legal regulation of services. In the United Kingdom, the extent of this regulation has increased since the 'big bang' despite the government's commitment to freedom. The Commission will establish basic rules to protect depositors, investors and policy-holders. There will be a set of minimum safeguards in the Community. When these ground rules are in operation then the providers of public services will be able to operate in any of the member states.

There has been a basic right of establishment for banks since 1977. In addition, a number of directives has already been proposed, which, if agreed, will establish a minimum standard of harmonisation of supervisory criteria. If an institution satisfies these criteria in one state, it will be able to operate in the other states without further permission being required. A similar provision will relate to mortgages.

Some directives have already been agreed and dates set for their implementation. For example, from October 1989 one will establish minimum requirements for authorising unit trusts and their equivalents. Once authorised in one state, the trust will be able to operate anywhere in the Community. This directive applies to any 'undertaking for collective investments in transferable securities'. Other agreed directives refer to the publication of prospectuses for companies and official stock exchange listings. Eventually, the system of directives in this field will create a common minimum standard relating to new issues of securities to the public. The aim is to use the same documentation everywhere without having to get approval from each state. There will also be directives to enable credit institutions accepted in one country to establish themselves in all member states without further permission, provided that they follow local rules in the conduct of their business. These non-banks will need to meet minimum standards guaranteeing that their capital is sufficient.

Insurance Services

The United Kingdom is the major supplier of international insurance services although its relative importance and lead have diminished. The City of London, therefore, has a great vested interest in the nature of changes in the Community rules relating to insurance services. There is already a freedom of establishment for a company in any member state, but it must follow local laws and do business on the same basis as national companies. The main current problems relate to cross-frontier insurance. Most members except the United Kingdom impose restrictions which mean that an insurer in one state cannot underwrite risks in another state, except through a locally established branch or agency. This system is a handicap to commercial bodies looking for the most competitive premiums.

Major changes have already been agreed since the non-life insurance services directive was adopted in June 1988. This enables insurers to cover the risks of potential policy-holders in any member state irrespective of where the insurer is established. The result will be a liberalisation of the market for large industrial and commercial risks, including marine, aviation and transport risks. The United Kingdom specialises in these areas and stands to gain from the freeing of the market. Spain, Portugal, Greece and Ireland have been given a modified timetable for implementation of the directive which is scheduled for 31 December 1992. Spain will conform by 1997 and the others by 1999.

The other main type of insurance concerns life assurance. The Commission is working on a directive which is intended to be implemented by the end of 1992.

Intellectual Property

The phrase 'intellectual property' is applied to patents, copyright, trade marks and industrial designs. Although there are international agreements on, for example, patents there are still great differences in national laws relating to these areas. These variations have a negative influence on trade between member states. The Commission, therefore, is establishing a Community-wide trade mark system with a single registration requirement and a unified appeals procedure. This will operate alongside national systems. It will not be possible to obtain a Community trade mark where it would conflict with a pre-existing national trade mark right.

The Commission is aiming at uniformity throughout the member states in respect of the conditions on which trade marks are obtained, held and protected. It also intends tackling the areas where technological change has created problems, namely, computer software, copyright, semi-conductor chips and biotechnological inventions. There is also a whole range of proposals affecting copyright in general.

What Will Be the Effects of the Single Market on the Location of Industry and Commerce?

The answer to this question is a mixture of speculation and extrapolation from past trends. If past trends continue there will be a continued concentration of commerce, industry and wealth creation in the central, northern European area of the Ruhr, the Benelux countries, the Ile de France and southern England. This so-called 'power house' of the Community contains the main centres of government and administration, both national and Community. These naturally generate a large service sector and extensive tertiary employment. The transport and communications networks are geared to exploiting the concentration of population, wealth and employment.

Over a longer period of time it can be assumed that market forces will ensure some geographic expansion of this area. Labour and land will become relatively more expensive than on the peripheries. This should create a deterrent effect pushing new firms and the expansion of existing firms to other areas.

Two other major factors will help to counterbalance the tendency to concentration in northern Europe. The first is the European Regional Development Fund (ERDF) which, depending on how it is administered, should put more funds into the disadvantaged, peripheral regions such as parts of Spain, Ireland, Portugal, Greece, southern Italy, Wales and Scotland. Linked to this will be the Integrated Mediterranean Programmes. The ERDF will rise from £5 billion in 1987 to £9 billion in 1992. The plan is to double the share of these 'deprived' areas and they will receive between 60 and 70 per cent of the fund. Portugal will receive even more assistance from a special five year industrial modernisation scheme.

The second factor that may offset the centralising tendency will be the transport improvement programmes, especially the railway modernisation and renovation schemes which will create a Europe-wide network of high speed railways for passengers and freight. Experience in France suggests that this will help to revitalise those areas touched by the new and improved routes. Germany is busy changing the orientation of its rail network from the present East–West to North–South. The old network was designed with military considerations in mind so that troops could be easily switched between eastern and western borders. The new orientation is helping to generate economic growth on a more even basis in Germany.

The great worry for the United Kingdom in this context is that its government has never shown any understanding of the potential of modern railways. It has concentrated on reducing public expenditure on public transport, including the railways, and has insisted that private funds be used for new developments such as the Channel Tunnel or that the money comes from British Rail's own resources. These are inadequate. European governments heavily subsidise their railways and are increasing their commitment. At the same time, the United Kingdom government is cutting its allocation for railway subsidies. There is a serious risk that this blinkered approach will leave the peripheral regions of the United Kingdom cut off from the benefits of the continental railway system. These benefits will stop at the London terminals of the Channel Tunnel link and not continue to the North, West or South West. Track and rolling stock modifications are needed to operate continental standard trains on British lines. Cheap, fast and efficient rail links are essential if the United Kingdom's outlying regions are to compete in Europe.

There is a third element which will affect the location of industry, that is the price of labour. The labour force in some areas of Europe may be regarded as cheap in comparison with others, including Japan. If the problems of training can be overcome then this makes them attractive for 'screwdriver' plants which assemble and package products that are designed and researched elsewhere. This has already happened on a significant scale in the United Kingdom with the influx of Japanese assembly plants. They train the workers very effectively for their limited tasks and, using the latest high productivity technology, produce at low comparative cost. They do not, however, bring research and development and design employment with them. These plants therefore remain as classic expendable branch factories, easily contracted, expanded, or closed as market whim dictates. If the overall level of costs and wages rise in the United Kingdom, this type of plant can easily be moved to set up in lower cost countries such as Portugal or Greece. The pessimistic conclusion here is that cheap labour may be only a temporary attraction. In the long run location is supposed to depend upon the overall comparative costs of an area compared with others. In theory, areas are competing with each other for the location of firms, offering them a variety of natural and acquired advantages. Also, in theory, the industries are competing with one another for the factors of production in an area. The most profitable industry can buy more of the factors it needs. In so far as this applies in practice, the United Kingdom must ensure that it has a well-educated, trained, skilled and adaptable labour force and minimum costs of transport and distribution. There are many imperfections in the markets for factors and the location of industry is affected by many influences not covered by the simple theory. The Japanese, for example, tend to favour the United Kingdom for locating their plants because of the language, among other things.

Gaps in Policy

There is a tendency to believe that the Community has policies for all areas of human endeavour but this is certainly not the case. It has, for example, very little to do with defence. History has left this function with the Western European Union and NATO. It is making slow and stumbling steps towards a common foreign policy in appropriate spheres, but there is a very long way to go before we can talk of a 'Community foreign policy'. There are, moreover, many very important economic functions which remain the prerogative of national governments and which are only affected at their peripheries by Community policies. An example of this is the control of unemployment. Some policies, such as that which is slowly emerging on monopolies and mergers, are largely in the hands of members' own legislators and administrators with the Community laws only coming into effect after certain thresholds are reached. Some policies are still very much in the melting pot and the system of compromise that is endemic in the Community will ensure that there is as much diversity as uniformity in practice. This is likely to be the case with the social policy that eventually emerges.

Conclusion

The European Community has changed significantly since its inception in the 1950s. Its change of name from the European Economic Community (EEC) or the Common Market to European Community is, in itself, of note. It marks a shift in underlying attitude. The word Community involves an acceptance of a social as well as an economic dimension. It implies a working together towards common objectives rather than competition. The maturing of the European Parliament and the introduction of qualified majority voting in the Council of Ministers on a range of issues will ensure more democratic participation and more effective decision-making. The pace of change may quicken. If the intentions of the Single European Act are realised, the Community will become the world's largest and richest trading and political grouping. This could be achieved whilst maintaining very much the same degree of national diversity as exists at the moment. There is bound to be some trend towards greater uniformity because that is one of the effects of better communications, modern technology and economies of scale. Diversity tends to flourish in isolation. Uniformity tends to be part of the price of knowledge and communication. The hope is that a large degree of this uniformity is based on the adoption of the best standards and practice and not on the second rate.

There are alternative visions of the future. These have been expressed by M. Rocard, the French Prime Minister. He said, in April 1989, that two conceptions of Europe confronted each other. The first was Mrs Thatcher's 'Europe of the jungle, a house open to the four winds, a plane without a pilot'. The second was a vision of a

Europe of free exchange and economic competition, but with ground rules.

The lesson of history is that human society needs ground rules although these may require to be altered over time. Europe is passing out of the phase of the dominance of the nation state and entering the era of cooperative decision-making. The modern European experience in consensus and coalition politics within their own nation states will enable the transition to be accomplished more easily. It will be a matter of fortune whether the United Kingdom produces leadership capable of moulding our political system and attitudes to the new reality.

Index